Understanding

PROBLEM PROPHETIC PASSAGES

Volume I

The Olivet Discourse

D1564061

Understanding

PROBLEM PROPHETIC PASSAGES
Volume I

The Olivet Discourse

N.W. Hutchings

Hearthstone Publishing Ltd.

P.O. Box 815 · Oklahoma City, Ok 73101

A Division Of
Southwest Radio Church Of The Air

All scripture references are from the King James Version unless otherwise stated.

UNDERSTANDING PROBLEM PROPHETIC PASSAGES
First Edition, 1991
Copyright © by **Hearthstone Publishing**
Oklahoma City, OK

Printed in the United States of America

Published by:
Hearthstone Publishing
P.O. Box 815
Oklahoma City, OK 73101

ISBN 1-879366-10-X

Table Of Contents

Preface

Many Christians have problems with interpreting certain prophetic passages, because they try to force the interpretation upon the wrong people or the wrong time. In this first edition of this series of studies, we shall endeavor to provide the reader with an understanding of the Olivet Discourse.

At the time of the deliverance of this prophetic message to the apostles, they had finally come to an understanding that Jesus was indeed going away from them for a time. They had no idea whether He would be absent from their presence a week, a month, a year, or a millennium. It would appear, however, that they expected Him to return in their lifetime. Even as the Lord stood upon the Mount of Olives to return to Heaven, they asked, *". . . wilt thou at this time restore again the kingdom to Israel?"* (Acts 1:6).

A few days later Peter preached to the Jews in Jerusalem, *"Repent ye therefore, and be converted, that your sins may be blotted out, when the times of refreshing shall come from the presence of the Lord; And he shall send Jesus Christ, which before was preached unto you"* (Acts 3:19-20).

Were the apostles listening to the Olivet Discourse concerned about the church age or salvation by faith through grace for the Gentiles? Certainly not! Were those present at our Lord's ascension concerned about Gentile

1

salvation? No indeed! Were those listening to Peter mentioned in Acts 3 aware that Jesus Christ was crucified for the sins of the world? No! They were all interested in only one thing — restoring the kingdom of Israel. Matthew 24 provides us with prophetic signs, or evidence, when the restoration of the Kingdom of Israel is near at the literal return of Jesus Christ.

Introduction

In understanding the prophetic Word relating to the last days, the primary necessity is to first determine whether the prophecy concerns the church of the present dispensation, or Israel. Next, will the prophecy be fulfilled before the Tribulation, during the Tribulation, or after the Tribulation in the Kingdom age?

Of course, there is always disagreement among those who interpret Bible prophecy as to whether it is to be understood generally or specifically, symbolically or literally. Also, there is the problem of which prophecies are to be understood individually, collectively, or nationally.

Such problems in prophetic interpretations have led to eschatological divisions like pre-Millennial, A-Millennial, post-Millennial, pre-Tribulation, mid-Tribulation, and post-Tribulation.

In this first volume of *Understanding Problem Prophetic Passages*, we consider the Olivet Discourse in Matthew 24 and Luke 21.

Chapter One

The Gap Between
Two Mountains

"And as he sat upon the mount of Olives, the disciples came unto him privately, saying, Tell us, when shall these things be? and what shall be the sign of thy coming, and of the end of the world?" (Matt. 24:3).

"And he gathered them together into a place called in the Hebrew tongue Armageddon" (Rev. 16:16).

Mountains, when used symbolically in the Bible, are representative of governments. For example, we read in Daniel 2:35, *". . . the stone that smote the image became a great mountain, and filled the whole earth."* From the explanation of this part of King Nebuchadnezzar's dream concerning the course of world empires, we know that the great mountain that will one day fill the earth is the Kingdom of Jesus Christ at His second coming.

In our text we have two mountains, representative of two governments. In linear distance, only about fifty miles separate these two historical sites; but according to time, the gap between them has extended now for almost two thousand years. When Jesus answered the disciples' questions concerning the end of the age and His victorious return, He may have looked due north to the hill of Megiddo, where the armies of the nations will gather to oppose His return to bring the Kingdom of Heaven to this rebel planet Earth. This event will signal the end of the age and is the final sign of His coming. The end of Gentile rule over the Earth at the coming of the Messiah is predicted in at least one hundred different scriptures in the Old Testament, but perhaps Psalm 2:1-6 describes it best: *"Why do the heathen rage, and the people imagine a vain thing? The kings of the earth set themselves, and the rulers take counsel together, against the Lord, and against his anointed, saying, Let us break their bands asunder, and cast away their cords from us. He that sitteth in the heavens shall laugh: the Lord shall have them in derision. Then shall he speak unto them in his wrath, and vex them in his sore displeasure. Yet have I set my king upon my holy hill of Zion."*

THE MOUNT OF OLIVES

We read in 2 Samuel 15:31 that David and the loyal leaders of Israel covered their heads as a sign of shame, took off their shoes, and went up on Mount Olivet and wept. The reason for their sorrow was that Absalom had betrayed his father and led a rebellion against the government of Israel. This occasion looked forward to another great betrayal and rebellion, the betrayal of David's Greater Son, the promised King and Redeemer, by Judas Iscariot. Israel would rise up in rebellion and say, "We will not have this man to rule over us." The lament of David on Mt. Olivet was a sign that the kingdom promised by God was far removed by the violence and divisions that arose.

After David died, his son Solomon ascended to the throne. Solomon was wise and faithful to God in his youth, and he was even permitted to build the temple, the Lord's house. It would appear that the kingdom was indeed nigh at hand, but Solomon departed from the faith, took heathen wives, and sinned willfully against God. He cut down the olive trees on Mt. Olivet, which were a sign of spiritual Israel, and we read in 1 Kings 11:6-8, *"And Solomon did evil in the sight of the Lord, and went not fully after the Lord, as did David his father. Then did Solomon build an high place for Chemosh, the abomination of Moab, in the hill that is before Jerusalem* [Olivet]*, and for Molech, the abomination of the children of Ammon. And likewise did he for all his strange wives, which burnt incense and sacrificed unto their gods."* Because the idols of heathen gods replaced the olive trees on Olivet, the mount became known as "the hill of corruption." God divided the nation, and the messianic kingdom was removed even further away on God's timetable. Thus, we begin to see that important governmental changes in Israel have always been closely associated with the Mount of Olives.

In Nehemiah 8:15 it is related that after the return of the Jews from the Babylonian captivity, there was again an abundance of olive trees upon Olivet, and they gathered branches from the olive and pine trees to make booths for the Feast of Tabernacles. The symbolic meaning of this feast was that the wandering Jew had come home. The temple had been rebuilt, and the Levites again went up and gathered olives to make holy oil for the eternal flame to light the table of shewbread, representative of that Bread of Life who would come down from Heaven.

We read in Galatians 4:4-5, *". . . when the fulness of the time was come, God sent forth his Son, made of a woman, made under the law, To redeem them that were under the law, that we might receive the adoption of sons."* The association of the Mount of Olives with the ministry of Jesus to Israel was filled with meaning concerning His offer of the messianic kingdom. An imposter would have overlooked such a historic connection hidden in Scripture, but not the Son of God. In John 8:1-2, it is recorded that early in the morning Jesus went up on Olivet, and from there He went directly to the temple. It was then that the scribes and Pharisees brought to him the woman taken in adultery. Since none of them could cast the first stone because they themselves were sinners, Jesus told the woman, *"Go and sin no more."* After that He said, *". . . I am the light of the world: he that followeth me shall not walk in darkness, but shall have the light of life."* Jesus signified that He had indeed come to bring a spiritual regeneration and take away their sins, but because they would not accept Him as the Messiah, He said in verse 24, *". . . if ye believe not that I am he, ye shall die in your sins."*

In Matthew 21:1-2, Jesus and two disciples were upon the Mount of Olives, and He sent them to find an ass for Him to ride into Jerusalem to present His claim to the throne of David. This action was to fulfill the prophecy of Zechariah 9:9, *"Rejoice greatly, O daughter of Zion; shout, O daughter of Jerusalem: behold, thy*

King cometh unto thee: he is just, and having salvation; lowly, and riding upon an ass, and upon a colt the foal of an ass." From the Mount of Olives He rode into Jerusalem to the temple to fulfill Malachi 3:1, *". . . the Lord, whom ye seek, shall suddenly come to his temple. . . ."* Jesus then went into the temple, cast out the moneychangers, and answered questions and charges concerning His claim as the Messiah, brought by the chief priests, Pharisees, Herodians, scribes, and lawyers. These groups controlled the political and religious affairs of Israel, and each one categorically rejected Him as the promised Messiah. Jesus pronounced eight woes upon that generation while yet in the temple, and His concluding remarks are recorded in Matthew 23:38-39, *"Behold, your house is left unto you desolate. For I say unto you, Ye shall not see me henceforth, till ye shall say, Blessed is he that cometh in the name of the Lord."*

Jesus went out of the temple and predicted its complete destruction, and then He went back up on the Mount of Olives and sat down. We may wonder why Matthew noted the fact that the Lord "sat" upon Olivet, and the answer is provided in Zechariah 14:3-4, *"Then shall the Lord go forth, and fight against those nations, as when he fought in the day of battle. And his feet shall STAND in that day upon the mount of Olives, which is before Jerusalem on the east, and the mount of Olives shall cleave in the midst thereof toward the east and toward the west, and there shall be a very great valley. . . ."* According to the prophetic timetable concerning the coming of the Messiah to take the government upon His own shoulders, when Jesus left the temple and went to the Mount of Olives, it was time for the mountain to split in the middle, and also time for the destruction of the enemies of Israel. But Jesus had been rejected as Lord and King, so instead of standing, as Zechariah prophesied, He sat down in an attitude of resignation to the fact that the kingdom had been set aside because of the hardness of the people's hearts.

In Matthew 26:26-30 the events of the Passover that Jesus shared with the apostles in the Upper Room are recorded. Verses 29 and 30 provide us with a description of the concluding events: *"But I say unto you, I will not drink henceforth of this fruit of the vine, until that day when I drink it new with you in my Father's kingdom. And when they had sung an hymn, they went out into the mount of Olives."* The words of Jesus and their departure to the Mount of Olives looked forward to the day when Christ will return, the sins of Israel will be taken away, and the kingdom will be brought in, as described by Paul in Romans 11:26-27, *"And so all Israel shall be saved: as it is written, There shall come out of Sion the Deliverer, and shall turn away ungodliness from Jacob: For this is my covenant unto them, when I shall take away their sins."*

The last mention of the Mount of Olives in the Bible is in the first chapter of Acts, where Jesus ascended back to the Father. The site of the ascension again indicated that Israel as a nation would be left in their sins until the people as one cry out to Jesus at His second coming, "Blessed is he that cometh in the name of the Lord."

On the very top of the Mount of Olives today there is a hotel and other businesses, mostly Arab owned and operated, which stretch along the crest for the better part of a mile. On the side facing Jerusalem are thousands of graves and tombs. One section contains the tombs of the prophets (Amos, Hosea, etc.). It is believed, based on Scripture, that when the Messiah comes to Mt. Olivet, these will be the first graves to be opened in the resurrection; thus, the reason for these burial sites on that location.

The olive trees on Mt. Olivet today are at the lower elevation adjacent to the Kidron Valley in the Garden of Gethsemane. Olive trees never die; they continually spring up from the roots, and the ones in Gethsemane were probably there when Jesus stopped to rest before making the climb over the mountain on the way back to Bethany. These olive trees bear witness to Israel that Jesus Christ is the only Hope and their true Messiah.

THE MOUNT OF MEGIDDO

In considering the second mountain in this prophetic study, the Mount of Megiddo, we read of the gathering of the armies of the world to oppose Jesus Christ at His second coming in Revelation 16:14-16, ". . . *the spirits of devils, working miracles, which go forth unto the kings of the earth and of the whole world, to gather them to the battle of that great day of God Almighty. Behold, I come as a thief. Blessed is he that watcheth, and keepeth his garments, lest he walk naked, and they see his shame. And he gathered them together into a place called in the Hebrew tongue Armageddon."*

Why would the Devil gather the armies of all nations to fight the Lord Jesus and the armies from Heaven at this particular spot? The answer is readily provided by the biblical and historical accounts of the wars that have been waged in the valley of Megiddo, which stretches out from the foot of the mountain. Armageddon in the Hebrew language means "the mount of Megiddo, the mount of slaughter." The valley, or plain of Megiddo, extends from the Mediterranean Sea to the Jordan River. It has been from here that Satan has sent evil spirits to bring the kings of Earth and the mighty men to destroy Israel and fight against God. We read in Judges 5:19-20, *"The kings came and fought, then fought the kings of Canaan in Taanach by the waters of Megiddo . . . They fought from heaven; the stars in their courses fought. . . ."* It is evident that there were beings other than flesh and blood involved in this attempt to destroy Israel. We read also in 2 Corinthians 35:22-23 that the good king Josiah was killed by the archers of Pharaoh Neco in the valley of Megiddo. It was at Megiddo that Gideon routed the huge army of the Midianites and Amalekites with only three hundred men carrying pitchers and lamps. It was here that Samson fought the Philistines and David slew Goliath. Many other battles between God's earthly people Israel and the enemies of God were fought in the plain surrounding Megiddo. When Napoleon stood upon the mountain of Megiddo and surveyed the length of the great valley that lay to the east and to the west, he made the comment that all the armies of the world could maneuver in that great plain. The general's remarks were certainly prophetic.

After the kings of the ten-nation confederacy, the kingdom of Antichrist, have destroyed the false religious system that will arise after the Rapture of the true church, the Beast will gather his own armies, and to this massive force will be added armies out of all nations. They will gather in the valley of Megiddo as the Lord Jesus Christ stands upon the Mount of Olives. We read in Zechariah 14:6-7 that the Lord will go forth from Olivet, and there shall be destruction in the valley of the mountains, *"And it shall come to pass in that day, that the light shall not be clear, nor dark: But it shall be one day which shall be known to the Lord, not day, nor night: but it shall come to pass, that at eveningtime it shall be light."*

In Revelation 19:19 we have described for us the opening phase of this greatest battle that will ever be fought in the history of the world, *"And I saw the beast, and the kings of the earth, and their armies, gathered together to make war against him that sat on the horse, and against his army."*

The outcome of this battle is a foregone conclusion. The armies of this world will be destroyed, and the Antichrist and the False Prophet will be cast into the lake of fire. We read in Zechariah 14:16, *"And it shall come to pass, that every one that is left of all the nations which came against Jerusalem shall even go up from year to year to worship the King, the Lord of hosts, and to keep the feast of tabernacles."*

As Jesus sat upon the Mount of Olives almost two thousand years ago, He told the apostles that before the battle of Armageddon would come, Israel must first be scattered into all the world because of their unbelief. As the prophet Hosea prophesied, *"For the children of Israel shall abide many days without a king, and without a prince, and without a sacrifice, and without an image, and without an ephod, and without teraphim"*(Hos. 3:4).

Today, as we see Israel back in the land from all nations, the rise of the revived Roman Empire, Russian involvement in the Middle East, the threat of the entanglement of the various blocs of nations in the Arab-Israeli wars because of the great need for oil, and many other prophetic signs that Jesus said must come to pass, we know the gap between Olivet and Armageddon is rapidly closing. We can already see the time spoken of in Joel 3:2, *"I will also gather all nations, and will bring them down into the valley of Jehoshaphat, and will plead with them there for my people and for my heritage Israel, whom they have scattered among the nations, and parted my land."*

Through wars and treaties, nations are still trying to take away or divide the land that God gave to the seed of Abraham through Isaac. As Christians see this happening before their eyes on television, they need to heed the words of Paul in Romans 13:12, *"The night is far spent, the day is at hand: let us therefore cast off the works of darkness, and let us put on the armour of light."*

Chapter Two

The Beginning Of Sorrows

"And as he sat upon the mount of Olives, the disciples came unto him privately, saying, Tell us, when shall these things be? and what shall be the sign of thy coming, and of the end of the world? And Jesus answered and said unto them, Take heed that no man deceive you. For many shall come in my name, saying, I am Christ; and shall deceive many. And ye shall hear of wars and rumours of wars: see that ye be not troubled: for all these things must come to pass, but the end is not yet. For nation shall rise against nation, and kingdom against kingdom: and there shall be famines, and pestilences, and earthquakes, in divers places. All these are the beginning of sorrows" (Matt. 24:3-8).

The twenty-fourth and twenty-fifth chapters of Matthew comprise what is commonly called by theologians the Olivet Discourse. This prophetic discourse by Jesus was prompted by two questions asked by His disciples as He sat down on Mt. Olivet. These two questions are:

1. When shall these things be?
2. What shall be the sign of thy coming, and of the end of the world?

The two questions asked by the disciples were the result of Jesus' reference to the destruction of the temple, and the benediction of His Temple Address, *". . . Ye shall not see me henceforth, till ye shall say, Blessed is he that cometh in the name of the Lord"* (Matt. 23:39).

There are only two question marks in verse 3, so there are only two questions. The signs of Christ's coming and signs of the end of the world mean the same thing. As far as the first question is concerned, we can all but eliminate it as far as the account of the Olivet Discourse recorded by Matthew is concerned. It is the general consensus of prophetic scholars that the first question is answered in Luke. Dr. J. Dwight Pentecost wrote on page 376 of *Things To Come: "The answer to the first question is not recorded by Matthew, but is given in Luke 21:20-24." Dake's Annotated Reference Bible* and many other sources I could quote give the same explanation. The reason we do not find the answer to the first question in Matthew is that he was commissioned by God to record the ministry of Jesus from the Jewish covenant position. As far as the dispensation of grace is concerned from an Old Testament projection, it always appears as a gap when looking forward to the messianic age. For example, in Daniel 9:26-27, the order of prophetic events for Israel leading to the kingdom skips from the cutting off of the Messiah and the destruction of Jerusalem to the Tribulation period, completely ignoring the dispensation of grace as though it would never be. Matthew, writing from a Jewish covenant relationship with God, does not infringe upon the church age. Luke had no such restrictions, so in his account of the Olivet Discourse he speaks of the "times of the Gentiles" and the treading down of Jerusalem. Therefore, we can consider all of the remarks by Jesus in Matthew 24 and 25 to be directed specifically to the time of His second coming.

Jesus signified by word and deed that He would relinquish His claim to this planet for a time, but that He would come again to reclaim it. So the disciples asked Him to give the signs whereby it might be known that His coming and the end of the world was near. The word in the Greek for "world" used here is *aion*, which means the end of the age, or the end of a generation.

The second place we find the word "world" used in Matthew 24 is in verses 13 and 14, *"But he that shall endure unto the end, the same shall be saved. And this gospel of the kingdom shall be preached in all the world for a witness unto all nations; and then shall the end come."* The word in the Greek for "world" used by Jesus here is not *aion*, but *oikoumene*, or "economy" in our English language. It includes the economic system of the world, but in the original text it means much more. The word "economy" in our text means all the inhabited world with all the systems of law, finance, government, and religion under which men live. The qualification in verse 14 means that in the end of the age — when the gospel of the kingdom is declared in all the world to all nations, races, and tongues, to men and women living under all kinds of governments and economic systems — whoever hears, believes, and endures to the end will be saved. Jesus Christ was referring to the peculiar economics of the Tribulation, when every person in the world will be called upon to work, buy, and sell using the mark and number of Antichrist. He who refuses this mark unto the end, even unto death, will be saved.

The third place we find Jesus referring to the world in the Olivet Discourse is in Matthew 24:21, *"For then shall be great tribulation, such as was not since the beginning of the world to this time, no, nor ever shall be."* The Greek word chosen here by our Lord to express precisely what He meant was neither *aion* nor *oikoumene*, but *cosmos*. *Cosmos* means not only the world, but the ordered and structured universe, the entirety of God's creation, the basic unit of which is the atom.

This time of tribulation that Jesus spoke of will not suddenly come upon the world. The Earth's inhabitants will not suddenly wake up one morning with the Antichrist sitting in the temple and his henchmen pounding on their doors demanding that they take his mark and number or be killed. This Great Tribulation was to be preceded by a time in which the generation of that day would be given many signs that this judgment was near and the return of Jesus Christ was imminent. Jesus called this time period preceding the Great Tribulation the "beginning of sorrows." There are seven specific signs that Jesus said would be given to men on Earth during this time period covered in our text. Seven is the number of completeness, and we shall consider them one by one in the order given.

SIGN NUMBER ONE — LIARS

Jesus said in Matthew 24:4, *". . . take heed that no man deceive you."* This means that in the last days men and women would distort the truth for gain and power. This sign is also set forth by Paul for the last days of the church age. Therefore, the last days of the church age and the time of the "beginning of sorrows" overlap. We read in 2 Timothy 3:1,13, *"This know also, that in the last days perilous times shall come . . . evil men and seducers shall wax worse and worse, deceiving and being deceived."* 2 Thessalonians 2:8-10 states, *"And then shall that Wicked be revealed . . . Even him, whose coming is after the working of Satan with all power and signs and lying wonders, And with all deceivableness of unrighteousness in them that perish, because they received not the love of the truth, that they might be saved."* We read in Revelation 13:14 that the False Prophet *". . . deceiveth them that dwell on the earth. . . ."*

God is truth; He cannot lie (Heb. 6:18). Satan is a liar; he cannot tell the truth (John 8:44). The more sinful and satanic a generation becomes, the more the lie is accepted as truth. Truth becomes what people want to believe. Such is the norm today.

A government agency has been established to monitor truth in advertising. No profit making company is going to spend millions advertising a lie that a certain dandruff shampoo will make men sexy and attractive to women unless it gets results. Millions lie in filing income tax returns, because it has become the smart thing to do. Government forms and thousands of investigators attempt to ferret out who is lying in order to receive welfare payments.

On the international front, good diplomacy involves which national representatives can tell the most believable lies. Since World War II Russia is given credit for breaking sixty treaties with the United States.

There have always been liars, but Jesus indicated that at the time of His return the masses would rather be deceived by lies than hear the truth. This general attitude by the unregenerate world is setting the stage for Antichrist who will deceive the world with "lying wonders" (2 Thess. 2:9).

SIGN NUMBER TWO — FALSE CHRISTS

In Matthew 24:5 Jesus said, *"For many shall come in my name, saying, I am Christ; and shall deceive many."*

There have always been world messiahs since the days of Nimrod, but why will there be so many in the last days? The answer is that as Jesus said, there will be wars, rumors of wars, crime, famines, diseases, earthquakes, social chaos, environmental problems, etc. The New Age promises a Maitreya; Islam is looking for the Mahdi; and the Jews are still looking for their Messiah. Messianic fervor is sweeping Israel to the extent that religious leaders are worried that rabbis are concerned they will receive a false Messiah. An article in the March 9, 1991 edition of the *Jerusalem Post* quotes Rabbi Schach as saying the temple will be rebuilt by 1993 to be ready for Messiah. The rise of false christs is being witnessed in all nations today.

SIGN NUMBER THREE — WARS

Jesus also said that during the time period called the "beginning of sorrows," *". . . ye shall hear of wars . . . For nation shall rise against nation, and kingdom against kingdom"* (Matt. 24:6-7).

In the course of human history, man has fought 4,535 wars, up to the last count, and 600 million men have been killed in these conflicts. Some people say, in regard to this particular sign of the end of the age, "Oh, we have always had war." However, Jesus was stressing that at the time liars and deceivers would increase, and an unusual number of false christs would arise, there would be a corresponding rise in the number and intensity of wars. Keep in mind that in all of history, 600 million people have been killed in war, and compare this statistic with the fact that half of these — 300 million casualties — have been in wars which occurred in the twentieth century. In other words, there have been as many people killed in war since 1914 as in the previous fifty-five hundred years. World War I and World War II eclipsed all previous wars in intensity, scope, and destruction. Today, without success, our diplomats are working feverishly to prevent World War III.

It is evident that when Jesus spoke of nation rising against nation and kingdom against kingdom, He was not simply declaring the obvious, but pointing to something that would occur at the end of the age. Sign number three has appeared as Jesus declared, providing additional evidence that we are living in the time of the "beginning of sorrows."

SIGN NUMBER FOUR — RUMORS OF WARS

Jesus said that at the end of the age there would be world wars, and He provided an additional sign by saying there would be rumors of wars. In other words, the minds of men would be continually on war, and war would be used as a psychological weapon. In 1 Thessalonians 5:2-3, Paul said that when the Day of the Lord would come, and the Tribulation night fell, people would be talking about peace and safety even as destruction from war fell upon them. Every time we turn on the television or see the latest newspaper, there are reports of a new war, or a new war rumor.

It would appear that man has spent more hours in peace negotiations since the United Nations was established than in all of history previous to that time. Think of all the hours spent in peace conferences in Geneva, Paris, Camp David, Peking, Moscow, Cairo, Jerusalem, and in almost every nation. The United Nations was formed as a result of the fear of war and a world cry for peace, but there is no peace. The nations will surrender their sovereignty to a world ruler who will promise peace, but sudden destruction will come in accordance with God's Word. The great fear of war and efforts to bring peace in our generation are just another sign Jesus gave that we are living in the "beginning of sorrows."

SIGN NUMBER FIVE — FAMINES

The fifth sign that Jesus gave concerning a definite time period in the last days which He called the "beginning of sorrows" was famines. We agree that there have always been famines, but as with the appearance of all the other signs in the last days, Jesus was not speaking of the ordinary course of human affairs. He was referring to a time of world famines that would surpass anything known before.

Over half of the world's population today lives in cities, solely dependent upon transportation and delivery systems for food and water. Only about five percent of the population in the United States even bothers to plant a garden; therefore, they have to depend entirely upon the local supermarket. This fact should strike horror at the thoughts of a war that will interrupt communications and transportation.

Famine is claiming millions in Africa, India, Iraq, and now even Russia fears massive starvation. Scenes on nightly television show relief teams attempting to get food to starving people around the world. Such reports are increasing, and will increase, until Jesus Christ returns and the deserts blossom as the rose.

SIGN NUMBER SIX — PESTILENCES

Jesus also said of the last days that great pestilences would arise. Of course, there have always been plagues, such as the bubonic plague that swept through Europe during the Middle Ages, smallpox epidemics, and we could mention many other deadly diseases that have been the scourge of mankind. Many point to the terrible flu epidemic that killed thousands, and perhaps hundreds of thousands during World War I, as a fulfillment of this particular sign. Today we have the spread of venereal diseases, a curse of God upon mankind for exceeding sinfulness. But even so, there must yet appear disease epidemics of such proportions that they will eclipse all these plagues. Disease epidemics always follow in the wake of famines. What if 100 million people in just India alone die of starvation? This would be equal to all the people in the United States west of the Mississippi River starving to death. We cannot begin to imagine the carnage, the filth, the contamination, and the spread of deadly diseases that would result. There would not be enough doctors or vaccination serum in the world to fight it. When we consider thirty or forty nations that have been added to the famine prospect list, the end results become staggering.

We must also consider the possibility of bacterial bombs in the arsenals of the nations of the world that will spread diseases and death over the face of the Earth. For example, there is one type of toxin called *Bacterium Clostridium Botulinum-Type A*. Just one of these bacteria organisms will kill a man, and only fourteen ounces (less than one pound) would be sufficient to eliminate the entire population of all nations.

There is also a secondary ominous message in the warning of Jesus relating to disease epidemics in the last days. Our Lord said that His return would be as the days of Noah, and we read that only Noah was perfect in his generation. We know that Noah was not perfect in the sense of sinless perfection, because he required God's grace (unmerited forgiveness). There must have been an unholy contamination of all flesh, with the exception of Noah and his household. We get a glimpse of this probability in 2 Peter and Jude.

The virus that causes herpes came in the wake of the sexual revolution of the 1960s. Then the HIV virus that results in AIDS appeared in male perverts in the wake of the homosexual revolution in the late 1970s. According to a recent U.S. Department of Health report, now twenty percent of all whites and sixty-eight percent of all blacks carry the herpes virus. On a world basis, estimates now run as high as 40 million with the AIDS virus. No one to this date has survived more than five years with AIDS.

No one can intelligently deny that in these days there are unheard-of disease epidemics.

SIGN NUMBER SEVEN — EARTHQUAKES

The seventh and final sign that Jesus mentioned in the first division of the Olivet Discourse was earthquakes. He said, *". . . there shall be . . . earthquakes, in divers places. . . ."*

According to published statistics, in the fifteenth century there were 150 recorded earthquakes; in the sixteenth century, 153 earthquakes; in the seventeenth century, 378 earthquakes; in the eighteenth century, 640 earthquakes; and in the nineteenth century, there were 2,119 recorded earthquakes. Statistics further indicate that in the twentieth century there will be more recorded earthquakes than in the past five thousand years. There have always been earthquakes, but Jesus was referring to an outbreak of earthquakes all over the world.

We would readily admit that part of the rate of increase in recorded earthquakes is due to improvements in scientific methods of detecting and recording tremors. But this factor in no way discounts the statistics that earthquakes are increasing in both number and intensity. Since 1917 the earthquake rate per year has climbed steadily. Of the eleven greatest known earthquakes in history, eight have occurred in the twentieth century, and we still have nine years to go. In Ezekiel 38 and in

Revelation, we read of the great earthquakes that are yet to come. Revelation 16:18,20 says, "*. . . and there was a great earthquake, such as was not since men were upon the earth, so mighty an earthquake, and so great . . . And every island fled away, and the mountains were not found.*" We read also in Hebrews 12:26, "*. . . Yet once more I shake not the earth only, but also heaven.*"

Yes, Jesus said that in the last days there would be earthquakes in divers places, and He said that all seven signs mentioned in the first division of the Olivet Discourse would be warnings that the time of the "beginning of sorrows" was upon the world, and the Great Tribulation was at hand.

Jesus said of these signs, "*. . . when ye shall SEE all these things, know that it is near, even at the doors*" (Matt. 24:33). On television we actually see WARS. The Persian Gulf conflict in early 1991 was called the "television war." Even every RUMOR OF WAR is reported. And, we actually see EARTHQUAKES like the World Series earthquake in San Francisco, and we actually see men and women dying of FAMINE and AIDS.

Surely, all these things are warnings that this world is on the very brink of the approaching Great Tribulation.

WHAT ARE YOUR CHANCES?

Some may say that they have heard these things all their lives; there has always been war, famine, and earthquakes. But Jesus gave seven definite signs, and the chance for all these signs to appear at one time in the manner described by our Lord is only *1 in 823,543.* But consider this: in the entire Olivet Discourse, *Jesus gave twenty-four signs*, and the chances of their coming to pass within a generation and in the order given is only *1 in 191 quintillions*, which is 191 followed by eighteen zeros. Thus, if you don't believe that we are living in the end of the age, and you are putting off your salvation, think of the odds against you.

In 2 Thessalonians 1:7-10 we read that God will save all who obey the gospel from the Great Tribulation, and the way to obey the gospel is by believing that Christ died for sins, and receiving Him into your heart as Lord and Savior.

Chapter Three

The Abomination Of Desolation

"All these are the beginning of sorrows. Then shall they deliver you up to be afflicted, and shall kill you: and ye shall be hated of all nations for my name's sake. And then shall many be offended, and shall betray one another, and shall hate one another. And many false prophets shall rise, and shall deceive many. And because iniquity shall abound, the love of many shall wax cold. But he that shall endure unto the end, the same shall be saved. And this gospel of the kingdom shall be preached in all the world for a witness unto all nations; and then shall the end come. When ye therefore shall see the abomination of desolation, spoken of by Daniel the prophet, stand in the holy place, (whoso readeth let him understand:) Then let them which be in Judaea flee into the mountains: Let him which is on the housetop not come down to take any thing out of his house; Neither let him which is in the field return back to take his clothes. And woe unto them that are with child, and to them that give suck in those days! But pray ye that

*your flight be not in the winter, neither on the
sabbath day: For then shall be great tribulation,
such as was not since the beginning of the world
to this time, no, nor ever shall be"* (Matt.
24:8-21).

In verses 4 through 7, Jesus gave seven signs whereby
His people at the end of the age might know that they
were living in the "beginning of sorrows." After the
beginning of sorrows, the world will go into the "time of
sorrows," and more specifically the "time of Jacob's
trouble," also called the Great Tribulation. The dispersion
and persecution mentioned by Jesus in verses 9 through
13 could be, and have been interpreted to be, the
scattering of the disciples, or the dispersion of all Israel in
70 A.D. But the setting given by Jesus for this prophecy is
not right for this interpretation. After the time period of
the "beginning of sorrows" has passed, then Jesus said
greater persecution will begin, and only those who endure
to the end shall be saved. The dispersion and persecution
mentioned by Jesus in Matthew 24:9-13 must be applied
to the scattering of the Jews by Antichrist mentioned in
Revelation 12:14-17, as the "man of sin" turns on all the
Jews who refuse to acknowledge him as Messiah. The
admonition in verse 13 to "endure unto the end" or be lost
is not for this dispensation. It is for the Tribulation. Any
Gentile or Jew who does not endure to the end, does not
refuse to take the mark of the Beast and worship him as
God, will be lost eternally in Hell (read Rev. 14:8-10).

In verses 16 through 21 of Matthew 24, Jesus speaks
of a future time when the Jews will suddenly have to flee
for their lives. The event that triggers this mass exodus

will herald a period of tribulation such as has never been known by man up to this time, nor ever will be again. The qualifying phrase given by Jesus to this prophecy is very important, "no, nor ever shall be." As great as the tribulation of the Jews in 70 A.D. was, it was not greater than the subsequent time of persecution. The purges and executions of Europe's Jews by Hitler greatly exceeded the sufferings of the Jews in 70 A.D. Therefore, we know this prophecy by Jesus referred to the future, a time that has not yet arrived, even though it is near.

This entire prophecy by Jesus centers around the event that will herald this greatest time of Jewish persecution, and bring great tribulation to all the world. We read again verse 15, *"When ye therefore shall see the abomination of desolation, spoken of by Daniel the prophet, stand in the holy place. . . ."* There are five things we need to know about the Abomination of Desolation:

WHERE WILL IT TAKE PLACE?

Jesus said the Abomination of Desolation that would herald the Great Tribulation, the last half of Daniel's seventieth week, was that which was spoken of by the prophet, and Daniel referred to this sacrilege thusly:

1. *"And he* [Antichrist] *shall confirm the covenant* [Israel's right to the land] *with many* [not all, but many] *for one week* [seven years]*: and in the midst of the week* [after three and a half years] *he shall cause the sacrifice and the oblation to cease, and for the overspreading of*

abominations he shall make it desolate . . ." (Dan. 9:27).

2. *"And arms shall stand on his part* [he shall worship the god of forces], *and they shall pollute the sanctuary of strength, and shall take away the daily sacrifice, and they* [his religious priests and the False Prophet] *shall place the abomination* [the image of the Beast] *that maketh desolate. And such as do wickedly against the covenant* [apostate Jews] *shall he corrupt by flatteries . . ." (Dan. 11:31-32).*

These prophecies forcefully declare that before Antichrist is revealed as "the man of sin," Jewish sacrificial worship must be restored in Israel. Jewish prayer books used since the dispersion in 70 A.D. contain prayers for the restoration of the temple, whereby the daily sacrifice might be restored. Since 1967, millions of Jews have stood at the Wailing Wall praying for the temple to be rebuilt and the sacrifice restored. Israel today is waiting for this hour.

Does this mean the temple must be rebuilt on the site where the Moslem shrine, the Dome of the Rock, stands today? Maybe yes, and then again, maybe not. In the New Testament there are three Greek words interpreted "temple." In thirty-five references, the word interpreted "temple" means the building, site, furnishings, the Holy Place, and everything else that was associated with the structure itself. In twenty-six references the word "temple" interpreted from the Greek means only the Holy Place, usually meaning the part where the Ark was located in the Holy of Holies. The tabernacle had a Holy Place beyond the veil, and the tabernacle was moved from place to place.

Some believe that it will begin the restored tabernacle of David on Mt. Zion that the Jewish sacrificial worship will be reinstituted during the Tribulation. This view is supported by two prophecies:

1. Amos 9:11: *"In that day will I raise up the tabernacle of David that is fallen, and close up the breaches thereof; and I will raise up his ruins, and I will build it as in the days of old."*
2. Acts 15:13-18: *"And after they had held their peace, James answered, saying, Men and brethren, hearken unto me: Simeon hath declared how God at the first did visit the Gentiles, to take out of them a people for his name. And to this agree the words of the prophets; as it is written, After this I will return, and will build again the tabernacle of David, which is fallen down; and I will build again the ruins thereof, and I will set it up: That the residue of men might seek after the Lord, and all the Gentiles, upon whom my name is called, saith the Lord, who doeth all these things. Known unto God are all his works from the beginning of the world."*

Thus, the Word of God states that after He has finished calling a people out of this world for Christ's name, meaning the completed church, the tabernacle of David will be restored. This means, of course, that the church age will end with the Rapture at the beginning of the Tribulation, and then the tabernacle will be restored. Again, there is a matter of opinion as to whether the tabernacle of David means the literal tent or the entire theocratic system.

We read in 2 Thessalonians 2:1-9 that before Jesus Christ returns, the Antichrist will sit in the temple of God, committing the Abomination of Desolation. But the Greek word used in 2 Thessalonians 2:4 is not "temple," meaning a building, but "Holy Place." In Revelation 11 where John saw the restoration of Jewish worship during the Tribulation, the Greek word again is not "temple," but "Holy Place." In reference to the restoration of Jewish worship before Christ returns, the Scriptures are careful to avoid referring to a literal temple. According to Zechariah, the Messiah Himself will build the temple after He returns, but in our opinion it will not necessarily have to be built before that time. The Antichrist could commit the Abomination of Desolation in the tabernacle or in some other structure in Jerusalem that is dedicated to the Old Testament sacrificial worship. Some may disagree, but this is our understanding of the Scriptures.

WHEN WILL IT TAKE PLACE?

The Abomination of Desolation will take place at the middle of the Tribulation period. It will occur exactly three and a half years after the Antichrist signs a treaty with Israel, giving the Jews the right to all the land of Palestine, including the temple site. Daniel 9:27 confirms that in the middle of the seventieth week (of seven years) the sacrifice will be stopped and the Abomination of Desolation will take place. Daniel 12:11 declares that 1,250 days, or three and a half years according to the Jewish calendar of three hundred sixty days per year, after the sacrifice is taken away, the Lord will come and bring an end to the reign of the desolator. We read also in

Revelation 12:14 that from the time the Antichrist moves to destroy all Jews who refuse to accept him as the Messiah until the faithful are delivered and restored to the land will be a time, times, and a half a time, or three and a half years. A time on the Hebrew calendar was from one Passover to the next. We read in Revelation 13:5, *"And there was given unto him a mouth speaking great things and blasphemies; and power was given unto him to continue forty and two months."* Therefore, Scripture is plain in that the Abomination of Desolation will occur three and a half years after the Antichrist, a man who has gained a reputation as a great peacemaker, signs a peace treaty with Israel guaranteeing them the land for seven years. Israel and Egypt have already signed a conditional treaty, but the treaty mentioned by Daniel and referred to indirectly by Jesus will be a covenant agreed to by all of Israel's neighbors and ratified by an international agency of nations. Currently, our Secretary of State, James Baker, is trying to negotiate such a treaty.

WHAT IS THE ABOMINATION?

The Abomination of Desolation is comprised of two parts — the abomination and the desolation. We will consider first the abomination. Of course, the Bible speaks of many things that men and nations do that are abominations before the Lord. Rape, murder, lies, adultery, cursing — all these and many more sins that men commit are abominations to God. But what we are interested in here is: What is the greatest abomination to God? If you will trace down all the references to abominations in your concordance, you will find that the worship of idols and the defilement of the tabernacle and the temple were the greatest abominations that Israel could commit. The setting up of idols in the temple would, of course, be the supreme abomination, or the offering of unclean meat, and especially the meat of swine, upon the altar. The comparative degree of abominations before God is illustrated in Isaiah 66:3, *"He that killeth an ox is as if he slew a man; he that sacrificeth a lamb, as if he cut off a dog's neck; he that offereth an oblation, as if he offered swine's blood; he that burneth incense, as if he blessed an idol. Yea, they have chosen their own ways, and their soul delighteth in their abominations."*

The temple was called the Lord's house because it looked forward to the coming of the Lord to this place. As we read in Malachi 3:1, the Lord will come to His temple. The Holy Place is reserved for Jesus Christ, and if the high priest, or anyone, entered into it without blood, he was instantly killed. Even the man who tried to steady the Ark of the Covenant was killed. The ultimate abomination was to defile the Holy Place with sinful flesh. Josephus thought that Antiochus Epiphanes of Syria committed the Abomination of Desolation when he offered a sow on the altar, but Jesus, who lived about two hundred years after Antiochus Epiphanes, said it was still in the future. The Abomination of Desolation will be the appearance of the Antichrist in the Holy Place, claiming to be God, the Messiah. He will be seen by all people, probably over an international television network, and he will then receive a deadly wound while in the Holy Place. He will survive, according to Revelation 13:3-4. This will be the signal to place the image of Antichrist in the Holy Place, and everyone on Earth who refuses to worship the image as God will be killed (Rev. 13:14-15). The daily sacrifice will be taken away, because the Antichrist will claim to have offered himself as a sacrifice for everyone. He will counterfeit the atonement offered by Jesus Christ on the cross.

WHAT IS THE DESOLATION?

Desolation means utter waste, and we read in the Bible where God said He would make Egypt, Moab, Syria, Babylon, and other places and peoples who rejected Him, a desolation. The Abomination of Desolation means exactly what it implies. All people and all nations who refuse to worship the image of the Beast will be made a desolation. We read of the desolation that will come upon many nations during the Tribulation in Ezekiel 29:9-12, *"And the land of Egypt shall be desolate and waste . . . No foot of man shall pass through it, nor foot of beast shall pass through it, neither shall it be inhabited forty years. And I will make the land of Egypt desolate in the midst of the countries that are desolate. . . ."* The Tribulation period, and especially the last half of the Tribulation, will be one great war, and we read of this time in Daniel 9:26, *". . . and unto the end of the war desolations are determined."*

We read about the extent of desolation in Revelation 16. The sea will become dead and lifeless, the rivers and wells will be polluted, cities will be literally flattened to the ground, and the grass of the meadows and the trees of the forest will be burned. This will be a time of desolation of three and a half years such as the world has never known. It will begin with the Antichrist committing the abomination in the temple or tabernacle in the Holy Place, when he demands that everyone in the world take his mark, number, or name, and worship him as God. No nation will escape, and this is why Jesus said in Matthew 24:15,21, *"When ye therefore shall see the abomination of desolation, spoken of by Daniel the prophet, stand in the holy place . . . then shall be great tribulation, such as was not since the beginning of the world to this time, no, nor ever shall be."*

WILL ANY SURVIVE THE DESOLATION?

Considering the judgments of the last three and a half years of the Tribulation, some may wonder if any will escape. But the Word of God is plain — some will endure to the end; some will escape so that the plan and purpose of God for this world will continue. Jesus said in Matthew 24:22, *"And except those days should be shortened, there should no flesh be saved: but for the elect's sake those days shall be shortened."* A third of the Jews will escape to a hiding place prepared by God. We read in Zechariah 13:8-9, *"And it shall come to pass, that in all the land, saith the Lord, two parts therein shall be cut off and die; but the third part shall be left therein. And I will bring the third part through the fire, and will refine them as silver is refined, and will try them as gold is tried: they shall call on my name, and I will hear them: I will say, It is my people: and they shall say, the Lord is my God."* We read also in Zechariah 14:16, *"And it shall come to pass, that every one that is left of all the nations which came against Jerusalem shall even go up from year* to year to worship the King, the Lord of hosts. . . ."

As we see the Jews back in the land, we know that the Abomination of Desolation spoken of by Daniel and the return of the Lord Jesus Christ is near. We read these words of Jesus in Luke 21:36, *"Watch ye therefore, and pray always, that ye may be accounted worthy to escape all these things that shall come to pass, and to stand before the Son of man."*

Chapter Four

The Mark Of The Beast

"For then shall be great tribulation, such as was not since the beginning of the world to this time, no, nor ever shall be. And except those days should be shortened, there should no flesh be saved: but for the elect's sake those days shall be shortened" (Matt. 24:21-22).

In the third division of the Olivet Discourse our Lord Jesus Christ spoke of a time immediately preceding the "coming of the Son of man" when all mankind would be in danger of extinction, and unless God were to intervene, all human life on the planet Earth would come to an end. Therefore, the hope of this world is not in social, religious, or political processes, but rather in the hope of the second coming of Christ.

The most perilous period for mankind at the end of this age begins with the mark of the Beast. Our comparative scripture is Revelation 13:16-18, *"And he causeth all, both small and great, rich and poor, free and bond, to receive a mark in their right hand, or in their foreheads: And that no man might buy or sell, save he that had the mark, or the name of the beast, or the number of his name. Here is wisdom. Let him that hath understanding count the number of the beast: for it is the*

*number of a man; and his number is Six hundred,
threescore and six."*

THE NUMBER 666

The number six is the number of man. Man was
created on the sixth day, and God said that he was to
work six days out of seven. Seven is the number of
perfection, and six represents man as a sinner trying to
become his own god, or man in rebellion against his
Creator. There are six dispensations of time in the day of
man, but the seventh dispensation, which will be ushered
in with Armageddon, belongs to God, and it will be called
"The Lord's Day."

There are six names for a serpent (a symbol of Satan)
in the original Hebrew. Six times in the New Testament
Jesus was accused of having a devil. There are six major
false religions of man. Jerusalem was trodden down by
the Roman Empire for 666 years — from the time of the
battle of Actium in 31 B.C. to the Saracen conquest in 636
A.D. — and the Antichrist, whose number will be 666, will
rise up out of the revived Roman Empire.

The number six always brands men as enemies of
God. Goliath was six cubits in height, he had six pieces of
armor, and his spear head weighed six hundred shekels of
iron. The image of Nebuchadnezzar was sixty cubits high
and six cubits in width; the playing of music was the
command for all to fall down and worship the image as
their god, and the music was played upon six instruments.
In Goliath we have one six, connected with the pride of
fleshly power. In the image of Nebuchadnezzar we have
the remaining two sixes, representing the perpetuation of

man's dominion over the earth in opposition to the kingdom of Heaven. In the person of Antichrist we have three sixes, a trinity of evil, combining the might of man, the Devil, and the fallen angelic host, to exalt the throne of Satan over the throne of God.

In the past, many have attempted to identify certain political or religious personalities as the Antichrist, by determining the total numerical value of the letters in their names. Most ancient languages did not contain separate numbers like our own English language. The first lettter of the alphabet would represent one, the second letter two, and so on, until enough numerical values were assigned to express any given figure through combinations of letters. A publication entitled *Who Is The Antichrist?* cites the Smalcaid articles as quoting Martin Luther to the effect that he believed the pope of the Roman Catholic Church would be the Antichrist. I quote from this tract:

> *"The pope is called 'Vicarius Filii Dei' (the vicar of the Son of God). . . . The title 'Vicarius Filii Dei' . . . is the number of the beast. . . . Let us count it by Roman numerals. V equals 5; I equals 1; C equals 100; A has no value; R no value; I equals 1; U (or V in Latin are the same) equals 5; S no value; F no value; I equals 1; L equals 50; I equals 1; I equals 1; D equals 500; E no value; I equals 1. Add them up and you have 666."*

We ourselves have never attempted to identify the pope as "the" Antichrist. We have always believed that according to Scripture, he would be a Jew, or part Jew, and would rise up out of the revived Roman Empire of Western Europe, and gain a wide reputation as a peacemaker. In this respect we have pointed out the parallel between these qualifications and Dr. Henry Kissinger, our past Secretary of State, but we have never claimed that Dr. Kissinger would become the Antichrist. However, we have received many numerical designs by those who have figured out the value of Dr. Kissinger's name in accordance with their own devised method. For example, by assigning A the value of 1, B the value of 2, C the value of 3, and so on through all the twenty-six letters of our alphabet, and then by adding up the corresponding values in the letters of the name "Kissinger," you will arrive at a total of 111, and by multiplying this figure by six, we have the number 666. But as interesting as all the numerical identification systems of prominent personalities are, the identification of any one man by such systems in our day remains only a matter of interesting speculation.

THE MARK OF ANTICHRIST

The first man to receive a mark on his body was Cain. Cain was the representative sinner in six ways:

1. He offered a polluted sacrifice.
2. He committed murder.
3. He lied to God.
4. God marked him.
5. Cain went his own way.
6. He made a name for himself by building a city.

The mark that God put on Cain was to keep others from killing him, but all who do not receive the mark of the Beast during the Tribulation will be killed on sight by those who are appointed to enforce the will of the Beast upon the world. The sole exception will be the 144,000 Jewish witnesses for God during the Tribulation. They will bear a sign in their foreheads, but it will be the seal of God. We read of their sealing in Revelation 7:2-3, *"And I saw another angel ascending from the east, having the seal of the living God: and he cried with a loud voice to the four angels, to whom it was given to hurt the earth and the sea, Saying, Hurt not the earth, neither the sea, nor the trees, till we have sealed the servants of our God in their foreheads."* We notice that the seal in the foreheads of God's witnesses is not called a mark.

Taking a mark on a person's body originated with Cain. It was a sign that he willfully departed from God's plan of salvation. The Hindus have marked their bodies with religious emblems for thousands of years. Even today, the natives in Africa and South America bear scars of wounds inflicted deep in their flesh as religious signs relating to demonism and Devil worship. God commanded in Leviticus 19:28, *"Ye shall not make any cuttings in your flesh for the dead, nor print any marks upon you: I am the Lord."* While we may not know what the design of the mark of the Beast during the Tribulation will be, it will certainly identify all those who have turned from God to accept and worship Satan's man, the Antichrist, as their lord and god. This is why the warning to everyone living during the Tribulation is given in Revelation 14:9-10, *". . . If any man worship the beast and his image, and receive his mark in his forehead, or in his hand, The same shall drink of the wine of the wrath of God, which is poured out without mixture into the cup of his indignation; and he shall be tormented with fire and brimstone in the presence of the holy angels, and in the presence of the Lamb."*

THE NAME OF ANTICHRIST

We notice in Revelation 13:17 that another requirement for those living during the Tribulation in order to buy, work, sell, and save their lives, will be to take the name of Antichrist. Every rebel of God's plan and purpose for man and the world has sought to make a name for himself. We read of those who rebelled against God at Babel, *"And they said, Go to, let us build us a city and a tower, whose top may reach unto heaven; and let us make us a name . . ."* (Gen. 11:4). Man's making himself a name indicates pride in his own works, the same pride that drove Cain away from God.

The Antichrist will seek to glorify himself above every other name in Heaven or on Earth. We read of him in 2 Thessalonians 2:4, *"Who opposeth and exalteth himself above all that is called God, or that is worshipped; so that he as God sitteth in the temple of God, shewing himself that he is God."* We have good scriptural reasons for believing that during the latter half of the Tribulation it will become illegal for anyone to have a name whereby he may be personally identified. Already, names are becoming obsolete. The June 1973 Penn State graduates received a yearbook that substituted digits for their names. I quote from the March 2, 1974 edition of the *St. Joseph News Press:*

". . . All signs point to a day, perhaps not far off, when money will go out of style. . . . Computerization is already well on its way to completely revolutionizing the banking business. Your signature on a check is now as obsolete as the use of beeswax to seal a letter. That string of incomprehensible letters in the bottom left hand corner of the check is the real you. . . . The banks naturally welcome the new day coming. . . . The government may be delighted, too. A recent federal law provides for electronically dispensed payments of welfare benefits to the needy, elderly, blind, or disabled. . . ."

A person's number is becoming more important than his name, and it is easy to visualize a day, in the not too far distant future, when personal names will be abolished; that is, every name except the name of Antichrist. When a man or woman accepts Jesus Christ as Lord and Savior, then they become a Christian. Likewise, because the Beast is an anti-type of Christ, all who accept his number and mark will also receive the name of Antichrist. This is what we are told in Revelation 13:17, and the Beast will seek to make only the name of Antichrist mentioned in all the Earth. But we read in Revelation 14:11, *". . . the smoke of their torment ascendeth up for ever and ever: and they have no rest day nor night, who worship the beast and his image, and whosoever receiveth the mark of his name."*

HOW NEAR IS THE MARK OF THE BEAST?

Dr. Henry Kissinger, according to an Associated

Press release that appeared in the *Houston Chronicle* dated May 5, 1976

> *". . . called for a new international economic order. He said, 'Our age, for the first time in history, has the technical capacity.' "*

On May 2, 1976, the United Nations General Assembly declared the establishment of a "New International Economic Order," which will include the "cancellation of all previous debts." Why worry about the billions that foreign nations owe our country? According to the United Nations, under the new economic order all debts will be cancelled. The new system would also take care of our own national debt. It looks good in print, but what would this do to your own personal bank account and savings? Would the individual receive one hundred percent credit for each dollar owned? Fifty percent credit? Twenty-five percent credit? Or nothing at all? How near is the day? We quote from an article entitled "Cashless Society Expected To Become Reality Soon" from the September 21, 1976 edition of the *Daily Oklahoman:*

> *"The long-talked about 'cashless society' is almost here. Bank debit cards are expected to go into nationwide use soon, and the U.S. Mint has recommended abolition of half dollars and pennies. . . . This (will) eliminate the need for statements, check writing, finance charges, envelopes, and postage. Maybe we can learn to get along without money. . . . Payment of bills*

by debit card is coming. Computer coded prices on items at supermarkets and bank debit cards will make it possible for customers to obtain groceries without seeing the money come or seeing it go. Changes are taking place and demanding such rapid adaptation of individuals that a new word has been coined to describe them — rapidation. . . . Scientists have reduced the size and cost of computers, so that countless uses have developed. . . . Why go any place or do anything, when you can send a computerized device to do it for you? Are we ready for this stage of electronic living? It's almost here."

An article in the January 19, 1991 edition of USA Today under the heading "Banks Hope To Stamp Out Paying By Check," states:

"Bankers hope to give the United States Postal Service a licking when it unveils the new 30-cent first-class stamp in February. . . . Last year, 29 million people representing thirty-two percent of the U.S.A.'s households paid 469 million bills electronically. . . ."

AT&T advertises the Universal Credit Card under the promise, "One World — One Card." It appears soon that all the world will be working, buying, and selling, using only computer code marks and numbers.

If we believe the Bible is the inspired and infallible Word of God, then we must also believe that God has set a day before the literal return of Christ to the earth in which everyone will have to worship the Antichrist as God in order to get their code and number. What the reader must decide is whether the coming cashless society is the same as the prophecy in Revelation 13. If so, then this generation stands on the brink of the Tribulation period.

Some have asked us whether they would be taking the mark of the Beast if they used the computer buying and selling system. Our answer is no, because as long as we are in the world we have to live somewhat by world economic standards. The mark of the Beast will come when a world dictator sits in the temple or tabernacle of God in Jerusalem (2 Thess. 2:4) and demands universal worship through the receiving of his own mark and number. However, we believe that according to 1 Thessalonians 4 and 5, Christians will be taken out of the world before this abomination occurs.

Nevertheless, the signs of our time indicate that the last days of this age are winding down. God does not want us to be ignorant of the fact that the day of Christ's return is at hand (1 Thess. 5:1-6). We must be about the Father's business, urging the lost to be saved through faith in Jesus Christ before that terrible day of darkness falls upon the earth.

We read of many who will live in the day of the mark of the Beast in Revelation 14:9-11, *"And the third angel followed them, saying with a loud voice, If any man worship the beast and his image, and receive his mark in his forehead, or in his hand, The same shall drink of the wine of the wrath of God, which is poured out without mixture into the cup of his indignation; and he shall be tormented with fire and brimstone in the presence of the holy angels, and in the presence of the Lamb: And the smoke of their torment ascendeth up for ever and ever: and they have no rest day nor night, who worship the beast and his image, and whosoever receiveth the mark of his name."*

The signs of the times, we believe, indicate that the day is near, even at the door. But God has provided another door. Jesus Christ said, as recorded in John 10:9-10, *"I am the door: by me if any man enter in, he shall be saved . . . I am come that they might have life, and that they might have it more abundantly."*

Each reader who is not assured that he has been born again by faith in Jesus Christ has two choices:

1. To believe on Jesus Christ who died for sin and be saved, or
2. To take the chance of dying in sin, or living to take the mark of the Beast during the coming Great Tribulation.

We have never known a person who said they were going to believe in Jesus Christ and be saved SOMEDAY, who ever really made the decision. This is why the Bible tells us, *". . . now is the accepted time; behold, now is the day of salvation"* (2 Cor. 6:2). Will this be your day of salvation?

Chapter Five

The Nations In God's Net

"For as the lightning cometh out of the east, and shineth even unto the west; so shall also the coming of the Son of man be. For wheresoever the carcase is, there will the eagles be gathered together. Immediately after the tribulation of those days shall the sun be darkened, and the moon shall not give her light, and the stars shall fall from heaven, and the powers of the heavens shall be shaken: And then shall appear the sign of the Son of man in heaven: and then shall all the tribes of the earth mourn, and they shall see the Son of man coming in the clouds of heaven with power and great glory. And he shall send his angels with a great sound of a trumpet, and they shall gather together his elect from the four winds, from one end of heaven to the other. Now learn a parable of the fig tree; When his branch is yet tender, and putteth forth leaves, ye know that summer is nigh: So likewise ye, when ye shall see all these things, know that it is near, even at the doors. Verily I say unto you, This generation shall not pass, till all these things be fulfilled. Heaven and earth shall pass away, but my words shall not pass away. But of that day

and hour knoweth no man, no, not the angels of heaven, but my Father only" (Matt. 24:27-36).

This fourth division of the Olivet Discourse deals the two signs:

1. The battle of Armageddon, where the birds will gather to eat the flesh of the armies of Antichrist, and
2. The refounding of Israel as a nation in the last days, as a sign that the "times of the Gentiles" would soon end.

Israel is the land wedge between Asia and Africa. Millions of birds darken the sky over Israel during times of migration in the spring and fall. Also, the ecology of Israel has been miraculously revived since becoming a nation in 1948. As promised in Joel 2:23 for regathered Israel, rainfall has increased by one-third since 1948. Hills are covered with trees. Ibex (biblical wild goats) and leopards roam the valleys, and an article in the May 1990 edition of the *Jerusalem Post* reported that the Israeli air force was grounded during the vulture hatching season to protect the eggs and young birds.

These are two more important signs which signify that man's journey to Armageddon is nearly over. Our reference scriptures are:

Zechariah 14:1-3, *"Behold, the day of the Lord cometh . . . For I will gather all nations against Jerusalem to battle . . . Then shall the Lord go forth, and fight against those nations. . . ."* Revelation 16:14-16, *". . . the spirits of devils . . . go forth unto the kings of the earth and of the whole world, to gather them to the battle of that great day of God Almighty. Behold, I come as a thief.*

Blessed is he that watcheth . . . And he gathered them together into a place called in the Hebrew tongue Armageddon." Revelation 19:17-19, *"And I saw an angel standing in the sun; and he cried with a loud voice, saying to all the fowls that fly in the midst of heaven, Come and gather yourselves together unto the supper of the great God; That ye may eat the flesh of kings, and the flesh of captains, and the flesh of mighty men . . . And I saw the beast, and the kings of the earth, and their armies, gathered together to make war against him that sat on the horse, and against his army."*

THE REBIRTH OF ISRAEL

The nation of Israel is represented by four plants within the context of scripture. Apostate Israel is spoken of as a bramble bush, spiritual Israel is represented by the olive tree, the vine is redeemed Israel, and the fig tree is national Israel. When Jesus cursed the fig tree and it withered and died, this was a sign that national Israel would cease to exist as an independent country within that generation to which He spoke. It happened in 70 A.D. when Titus finally broke through the walls of Jerusalem. But Jesus also said in the Olivet Discourse that the budding of the fig tree would be an important sign that the Great Tribulation was at hand and His coming was near. The budding of the fig tree could only refer to the rebirth of Israel.

As we have already brought out in these studies, Matthew was confined to God's covenant relationship with Israel and the messianic promises in recording the important events of our Lord's ministry. But Luke's gospel is expanded in scope to include the "times of the Gentiles," and we read the corresponding scripture in Luke 21:29-31, *"And he spake to them a parable; Behold the fig tree, AND ALL THE TREES; When they now shoot forth, ye see and know of your own selves that summer is now nigh at hand. So likewise ye, when ye see these things come to pass, know ye that the kingdom of God is nigh at hand."*

Trees, when used figuratively in Scripture, are always symbolic of nations, or the chief ruler of the nation (read Judges 9, Ezekiel 31). Luke said that after the budding of the fig tree, all the trees would shoot forth new buds. With the refounding of Israel in 1948, there came a surge of nationalism such as the world has never witnessed before. The French, Dutch, English, Spanish, Portuguese, and Belgian empires began to break up, and nation after nation rose up out of these empires and gained independent status. The United States granted independence to the Philippines, and all across Africa, the sub-continent of Asia, and the islands of the Atlantic, Pacific, and Indian oceans, new nations came into being. Therefore, not only the rebirth of Israel, but the birth of other nations in great numbers would be a sign that the day of man was coming to a close, and the Day of the Lord was about to dawn.

World utopian dreamers who promoted the breakup of the colonialism envisioned a day when all nations would sit in a common counciol and work together to promote peace, plenty, international good will, love, and brotherhood. But God's Word declared that this dream would turn into a nightmare. Joel 3:9-16 says, *"Proclaim ye this among the Gentiles; Prepare war, wake up the mighty men, let all the men of war draw near; let them*

*come up: Beat your plowshares into swords, and yrou
pruninghooks into spears: let the weak say, I am strong.
Assemble yourselves, and come . . . Let the heathen be
wakened, and come up to the valley of Jehoshaphat: for
there will I sit to judge all the heathen round about . . .
multitudes in the valley of decision: for the day of the
Lord is near . . . The Lord also shall roar out of Zion,
and utter his voice from Jerusalem; and the heavens and
the earth shall shake. . . ."*

The new nations have joined themselves into blocs
with the superpowers, and without social, political, and
agricultural guidance from their former governing nations,
they have only added to the frustration and poverty of the
world.

GOD'S CONTROVERSY WITH THE NATIONS

To understand what is happening among the nations
today, we go back to Genesis 10:5, *"By these were the isles
of the Gentiles divided in their lands; every one after his
tongue, after their families, in their nations."* Noah,
through his three sons, Ham, Shem, and Japheth, had
seventy grandsons. It was ordained by God that there
should be seventy nations upon the earth from the
grandsons of Noah. God ordained a place for Israel and a
place for Gentile nations. The reason that God willed that
mankind should be divided into races, nations, and
languages is explained in Acts 17:24-27, *"God that made
the world and all things therein, seeing that he is Lord of
heaven and earth, dwelleth not in temples made with
hands; Neither is worshipped with men's hands, as though
he needed any thing, seeing he giveth to all life, and*

breath, and all things; And hath made of one blood all nations of men for to dwell on all the face of the earth, and hath determined the times before appointed, and the bounds of their habitation; That they should seek the Lord, if haply they might feel after him, and find him, though he be not far from every one of us."

Today we hear much concerning a world currency, a world language, a world tribunal, and a world religion. President George Bush has stated repeatedly that the only way for mankind to survive the future is through a New World Order.

One-worldism, as advocated today, is a revision of the plan advanced by Nimrod at Babel. The world was saved from total extinction by eight souls who found grace in the eyes of the Lord. After the flood, God divided mankind into races, nations, and languages, and further divided them by boundaries — oceans, mountains, rivers, lakes, and by subsequent traditions, customs, and racial characteristics. God used geography, speech, color, racial abilities, and culture to keep the nations divided. He went to great lengths to keep the entire world from being corrupted by Satan as he had done before the flood when there were no nations or social and racial divisions. God would have some men and some nations that would be His witnesses to bear testimony before the world of His mercy and grace, that men might come to the knowledge of the truth and be saved. This will and intent of God is expressed again in 1 Timothy 2:1-6, *"I exhort therefore, that, first of all, supplications, prayers, intercessions, and giving of thanks, be made for all men; For kings, and for all that are in authority; that we may lead a quiet and peaceable life in all godliness and honesty. For this is good and acceptable in the sight of God our Saviour; Who will have all men to be saved, and to come unto the knowledge of the truth. For there is one God, and one mediator between God and men, the man Christ Jesus, Who gave himself a ransom for all, to be testified in due time."*

God looked down through the ages and saw the time when Satan would deceive the nations with another Babylonish scheme: The dictator of this world government would repeat the attempt made by Nebuchadnezzar to command all nations and peoples to worship his image as God or be killed. We read in Jeremiah 25:31-33, *"A noise shall come even to the ends of the earth; **for the Lord hath a controversy with the nations**, he will plead with all flesh; he will give them that are wicked to the sword, saith the Lord . . . evil shall go forth from nation to nation . . . And the slain of the Lord shall be at that day from one end of the earth unto the other end of the earth: they shall not be lamented, neither gathered, nor buried; they shall be dung upon the ground."*

Today Satan is stirring up the controversy between God and the nations. We read in Isaiah 14:12, *"How art thou fallen from heaven, O Lucifer, son of the morning! how art thou cut down to the ground, which didst weaken the nations."* Today Satan is weakening the nations through homosexuality, the sin that destroyed Sodom and Gomorrah. He is weakening the nations to prepare the way for the rise of a world government over which his own king, the Antichrist, will reign.

To illustrate again how near the world may be to this counterfeit kingdom, we refer you to the first fourteen verses of the twenty-first chapter of John. The scene described is by the Sea of Tiberias after the resurrection of our Lord. Eight of the apostles had been fishing all night with nets, but they had caught no fish. When Jesus appeared on the shore He instructed Peter to cast his net on the right side of the boat, and in verse 11 we read that they caught 153 fish.

There are no idle words in the Bible. All Scripture is given by inspiration and is profitable for doctrine, reproof, and correction, and the fact that John mentioned the exact number of fish must have an explanation. In the Bible, the gathering of the nations into the kingdom, over which God's Son will reign from David's throne, is compared to the gathering of fish in a net. For example, we read in Ezekiel 32:2-4, "... *take up a lamentation for ... Egypt ... thou camest forth with thy rivers, and troublest the waters with thy feet, and fouledst their rivers. Thus saith the Lord God; I will therefore spread out my net over thee with a company of many people; and they shall bring thee up in my net ... Then will I leave thee upon the land ... and will cause all the fowls of the heaven to remain upon thee. ..."*

God has said that He would bring the army of Egypt up in a net across their river (the Nile River), and leave them like a fish out of water in the open desert for the fowls to eat. This is another view of Armageddon. We read also in Matthew 13:47-49, "... *the kingdom of heaven is like unto a net, that was cast into the sea, and gathered of every kind: Which, when it was full, they drew to shore, and sat down, and gathered the good into vessels, but cast the bad away. So shall it be at the end of the world. ..."*

There are at least twelve scriptures relating to God's

catching up the nations in His net; therefore, it is evident that the 153 fish the apostles caught in their net indicates the number of nations there will be on earth when the Lord returns. The entire mass of humanity is referred to as a sea in the Bible. We read in Daniel 7:2, *". . . the four winds of the heaven strove upon the great sea. And four great beasts came up from the sea. . . ."* Revelation 13:1 says, *"And I stood upon the sand of the sea, and saw a beast rise up out of the sea, having seven heads and ten horns. . . ."* The beast referred to by John is the Antichrist and his empire that will rise up out of the sea, but also into the sea God will cast His net, and bring many fish, representing the nations, to Armageddon. The 153 fish mentioned in John 21 represent the number of nations in the world when Christ returns.

At the close of World War II there were fewer than one hundred nations in the world, but with the breakup of the colonial empires, the number began to rise. In 1966, when we first understood the meaning of the 153 fish caught by Peter and the apostles who were with him, we noted the count of nations had risen to 142.

The 1991 edition of the *World Almanac* lists the nations belonging to the United Nations at 159: 158 Gentile nations plus Israel. In John 21, Israel is depicted as the fish on the fire, and the Jewish people will be in the fire of the Great Tribulation. We read of this coming period of the greatest tribulation of Israel in Zechariah 13:8-9, *"And it shall come to pass, that in all the land, saith the Lord, two parts therein shall be cut off and die; but the third shall be left therein. And I will bring the third part through the fire, and will refine them as silver is refined, and will try them as gold is tried: they shall call on my name, and I will hear them: I will say, It is my people: and they shall say, The Lord is my God."*

The 158 Gentile nations listed in the 1991 *World Almanac* include East Germany which had already reunited with West Germany. There are other nations like South Korea also considering reuniting like West Germany and Vietnam. Also, the Antichrist will despose three rulers, probably taking national status from their countries (Dan. 7:8).

In the twenty-second chapter of 1 Kings we read that God had already determined how and where the wicked Ahab would be killed. We read in 1 Kings 22:20-22, *"And the Lord said, Who shall persuade Ahab, that he may go up and fall at Ramoth-gilead? . . . And there came forth a spirit, and stood before the Lord, and said, I will persuade him. And the Lord said unto him, Wherewith? And he said, I will go forth, and I will be a lying spirit in the mouth of all his prophets. . . ."* Ahab's prophets gave him bad advice. He went up to the battle and was killed, and the dogs licked up his blood. Today the apostates, the ecumenists, the liberal educators, the humanists, and the one-worlders are giving the nations bad advice. Lying spirits are working overtime (Rev. 16:13-16).

What is happening in Israel and the Middle East today is the beginning of the final act in the drama of the ages. God is catching all nations into His net, and the "times of the Gentiles" will be brought to an end. The goat nations will be judged during the kingdom age and cast aside, and seventy nations will remain, in accordance with God's plan and purpose from the beginning.

But before the Tribulation begins, the period of final gathering, the Lord will catch His people, the Christians, out of the world. Jesus stood on Mt. Olivet, looked into the future to Armageddon, and said to us today, *"And when these things begin to come to pass, then look up, and lift up your heads: for your redemption draweth nigh."* Are you, dear friend, ready for what lies ahead? If you have Jesus as your Lord and Savior, you will be ready, no matter what happens. Jesus died for the sins of all who will receive Him as Lord and Savior. Confess to God that you are a sinner, and ask Jesus to come into your heart.

Chapter Six

God's Prophetic Clock

"So likewise ye, when ye shall see all these things, know that it is near, even at the doors. Verily I say unto you, This generation shall not pass, till all these things be fulfilled. Heaven and earth shall pass away, but my words shall not pass away. But of that day and hour knoweth no man, no, not the angels of heaven, but my Father only. But as the days of Noe were, so shall also the coming of the Son of man be . . . Therefore be ye also ready: for in such an hour as ye think not the Son of man cometh" (Matt. 24:33-37,44).

The thirty-sixth verse of Matthew 24 is one of the most abused scriptures in the entire Bible. It is often quoted as a retort when anyone infers that the signs of the times indicate we may be living in the last days. To any mention of the second coming the usual response is that no man could know the day of His return; therefore, Christians are not to concern themselves with prophecy. Matthew 24:36 has become to the majority of church members today what 1 Timothy 5:23 — *". . . use a little wine for thy stomach's sake . . ."* — is to the alcoholic. Any scripture can be abused and misused when taken out of its proper setting and context.

In the first place, this qualification added by Jesus to end-time events could just as well apply back to the preceding verse concerning the passing away of Heaven and earth as it could to His second coming. In the second place, even if this statement has reference to His literal return, it must be understood in its Jewish setting, because the gospel of Matthew is Jewish. Spiritual blindness did come upon Israel, and that blindness will remain until Christ returns. In the third place, Jesus plainly indicated in verse 33 that those living in the last generation could know that His coming was near, even at the door. It is interesting to note that in Luke's account of the Olivet Discourse, which was recorded with a wider application to the "times of the Gentiles," he completely omits this qualification. In fact, Luke leaves the door of knowledge wide open concerning the coming of the Lord. Luke adds these personal exhortations: *"And when these things begin to come to pass, then look up, and lift up your heads; for your redemption draweth nigh"* (Luke 21:28). Luke also recorded Jesus as saying, *"So likewise ye, when ye see these things come to pass, know ye that the kingdom of God is nigh at hand"* (Luke 21:31).

In several of Paul's epistles, the apostle dealt with the closing years of the church age, and in every place where he mentioned the signs of the times that would precede the Lord's return, he set forth Christian responsibility to know by these signs that the end of the age was near. For example, consider 1 Thessalonians 5:2-4, *"For yourselves know perfectly that the day of the Lord so cometh as a thief in the night. For when they shall say, Peace and safety; then sudden destruction cometh upon them, as travail upon a woman with child; and they shall not escape. But ye, brethren, are not in darkness, that that day should overtake you as a thief."*

All references to Jesus coming as a thief in the night have application to

1. Spiritually blind Israel,
2. The unregenerate world at large, or
3. Professing church members.

Christians not only can know that the day of the Lord's coming is at hand, but they have a responsibility to know and to warn the unsaved that the day of God's wrath is near.

THE GENTILE IMAGE

We can know we are living in the end of the age from the second chapter of Daniel. Nebuchadnezzar dreamed of a great image whose head was gold, the breast and arms were silver, the belly and thighs were brass, the legs were iron, the feet were part iron and part clay, and the lower extremity of the image was represented by the ten toes of the feet. We are plainly informed that the head was Babylon, and then after Babylon the next world empire was Medo-Persia, called the silver empire. After Medo-Persia arose the Grecian Empire, and Greece gave way to Rome, the iron empire. Daniel 2:40 informs us that the Roman Empire would break up into pieces and bruise, which it did. The bruising of the pieces refers to the wars of Europe, and in the latter days, the two great world wars which were started among nations from the old Roman

Empire. But Daniel in verse 41 prophesied that in the last days, ten nations that originally broke off from the fourth kingdom — Rome — would come together and form an alliance.

After the breakup of the Roman Empire between 450 A.D. and 900 A.D., it continued to rule the world through the European colonial system (the Dutch, French, British, Spanish, Italian, Portuguese, Belgian, and German empires). The breakup of these empires has resulted in an increase in the number of nations. But out of this final breakup in the end of the age, the prophetic Word of God plainly foretells that ten nations would unite to form the revived Roman Empire.

In the January 1974 edition of *European Community* magazine, Willie Brandt, chancellor of the Federal Republic of Germany (at that time) is quoted as saying,

> ". . . *European union will come. . . . Our partners throughout the world regard European union as a future fact. . . . European union is to become a reality within this very decade. . . . The member states will transfer to the European government those sovereign rights which in the future can only be effectively exercised together.*"

In 1992 the European Common Market becomes one empire, born not out of conquest like the bigger beasts eating the smaller beasts, but out of common consent. *"These have one mind, and shall give their power and strength unto the beast"* (Rev. 17:13).

Had Napoleon had a united Europe behind him, he could have conquered the world; likewise Hitler. On a recent tour to the Middle East we picked up the June 1990 edition of *Atlas*, the magazine of the French Airlines. On page 140 in an article entitled "The E.E.C. In The World," this information is presented about the common European Empire:

☐ 7 percent of the world population
☐ 24 percent of the gross national product
☐ 44 percent of world trade
☐ 36 percent of currency reserves
☐ Capacity for savings equal to the U.S.A. and Japan combined.

We read of the revival of Rome into a ten-nation federation in Daniel 2:44, *"And in the days of these kings shall the God of heaven set up a kingdom, which shall never be destroyed. . . ."* We know that the hour is late on God's prophetic clock from what we see happening today in Europe.

ISRAEL, GOD'S HOUR HAND

God's greatest prophetic timepiece is Israel, and the promise of Israel's regathering began to be fulfilled with the Balfour Declaration in 1917. The Zionist organization recognized the document in 1918. We know from the Old Testament that God deals with Israel in definite periods of time, and in thirty years, from 1918 to 1948, Israel became a nation. Why thirty years? Because thirty is the Jewish age of maturity. Every fiftieth year in Israel was the year of Jubilee, the year of the restoration of land belonging to families. Fifty years from 1917, in 1967, Jerusalem was restored again to the nation. Before 1967, Israel had a new city of Jerusalem which they had built adjacent to the old Jerusalem, but the old city with the temple site was the city of peace recognized by God. The reclaiming of the old Jerusalem fulfilled the prophecy in Zechariah 12:6, *". . . Jerusalem shall be inhabited again in her own place, even in Jerusalem. . . ."* According to the prophet, the restoration of Jerusalem was to be in the latter times, just before the Messiah of Israel appeared.

We must also consider the restoration of Jerusalem as the fulfilling of another prophecy that has perplexed Bible scholars. We read, in Daniel 8, the first fourteen verses of the prophecy concerning the defeat of the Medo-Persian Empire by Greece, and how this prophecy would relate to Israel. Verse 13 says, *"Then I heard one saint speaking, and another saint said unto that certain saint which spake, How long shall be the vision concerning the daily sacrifice, and the transgression of desolation, to give both the sanctuary and the host to be trodden under foot?"* We know that in Daniel 9, the prophecy relating to the seventy prophetic weeks, each day represents a year. Charles DeLoach, author of *Seeds of Conflict*, gives the following interpretation to the prophecy of the twenty-three hundred days:

> *"The prophet Daniel said that the sanctuary or temple site, which God had given over to the Gentiles, would be returned to the Jews exactly 2,300 years from the date that the ram and the he-goat, symbols of two great empires, first met in battle. The prophet clearly identified the ram as the Medo-Persian Empire. The he-goat, he*

said, stood for the Greek Empire founded by
Alexander the Great. The first battle between
these two took place at the river Granicus in 334
B.C. From that date to the year 1967 A.D. equals
exactly 2,300 years. On June 7, 1967, the Jews
recaptured old Jerusalem and the site of the
sanctuary, thus fulfilling the vision."

In Israel today there is a growing messianic fervor, and with it an undercurrent of emotionalism to rebuild the temple . . . NOW! The Temple Mount Faithful have cut two cornerstones for the temple and have attempted to take them up to the Temple Mount. They say that in 1991 another cornerstone will be prepared, and then the Messiah will come and lay the fourth. Adjacent to the temple, devout Jews are busily making temple musical instruments to welcome the Messiah; priest's clothing are being prepared according to specifications; furniture is being painstakingly built according to scale; and Aaron's rod and a copy of the law is awaiting the Ark of the Covenant.

In an article in the March 6, 1971 edition of the *Jerusalem Post*, this information is given:

"Numerous examples and indicators of messianic
movement abound. . . . Using 1917 and the
Balfour Declaration as the starting point for the
Ingathering of the Exiles, the book of Daniel
predicted that fifty years after the Ingathering,
Jerusalem will be reunited (1967), to be followed
twenty-five years later by the reconstruction of
the temple. . . . The increase of Western sym-

pathy for Israel is also to be viewed in this messianic perspective. Rabbi Ashkenazi sees this as an increasing acceptance of Israel as the people slated to become 'a nation of priests.' Note that the more hostile Western countries — France and Italy — are essentially Catholic, while the friendlier ones — the U.S. and Britain — are Protestant. . . . Protestants have rid themselves of the idea that Christianity is the new Israel, while Catholics haven't."

Never before have pre-Millennial Christians and Orthodox Jewry been so close in eschatological understanding.

Some think that twenty years is a generation, and others say thirty or forty years. But we read in Psalm 90:9-10, *"For all our days are passed away in thy wrath . . . The days of our years are threescore years and ten. . . ."* It is evident that the God-established life span of man today is seventy years. We read in Jeremiah 7:29-30 that Israel would be in captivity in Babylon for a generation, and they were held captive in Babylon for seventy years. Jesus said that the generation of His day would see the temple destroyed, and He was speaking to people of His own age. The temple was destroyed by Roman soldiers in 70 A.D. Using 1918 as our beginning date for the budding of the fig tree, we count seventy years and come to 1988. The Balfour Declaration was accepted by Zionism in 1918.

The temple desecrated by the Antichrist will be destroyed, and the kingdom temple described in the last eight chapters of Ezekiel will be built by the Lord Himself.

Again, allowing seven years for the building of the Millennial temple, we would come to 1995. There is a calendar lag of four years, so 1995 would actually be 1999 A.D., or the year 5999 dating from creation. Allowing a year for the dividing of Israel by race, and restoration to their own tribal boundaries, we come to the year 2000 A.D. according to the Gentile calendar, or the year 6000 counting from creation. Six is the number of man, and God would have given man six thousand years to save himself and bring in his own heaven

GENERAL END-TIME SIGNS

In looking from Mt. Olivet to Armageddon, Jesus described for us living today the signs that we would see during the last generation. They are as follows:

1. Liars and deceivers
2. Wars
3. Rumors of wars
4. False messiahs
5. Famines
6. Pestilences
7. Earthquakes
8. Anti-Semitism
9. Betrayals of nation, faith, and family
10. Hatred increasing
11. Class welfare
12. False prophets
13. Lawlessness abounding
14. Love decreasing
15. Increase of gospel by mass communications

16. Refounding of Israel
17. Restoration of Jewish worship as established under the law
18. Abomination of Desolation
19. Great Tribulation
20. Rise of Antichrist the desolator
21. Flight of the Jews from Israel
22. Increased satanic powers
23. Mark of the Beast

According to my count we have already passed seventeen of these signs in this generation, and the remaining signs are to be fulfilled during the Tribulation period. The church could be raptured at any time. The hour hand on God's prophetic clock is approaching the midnight hour. Mankind is surging toward its rendezvous with the god of this world, Satan, on the plains of Megiddo.

There is a television commercial which attempts to attract a certain class of potential customer by declaring that their product is not for everyone. Likewise, God has declared that Heaven is not for everyone. There are those who make up their own minds that Jesus Christ died for their sins, and they escape from "the maddening crowd" by accepting Him as Lord and Savior. God has given you the opportunity to make up your own mind concerning what you will do with Jesus who is called the Christ. We read in John 3:16, *"For God so loved the world, that he gave his only begotten Son, that whosoever believeth in him should not perish, but have everlasting life."*

Chapter Seven

The Olivet Discourse Parables

Within the context of the Olivet Discourse in Matthew, Jesus used eight parables to further explain His teaching relating to the signs of His coming. In the context of the Olivet Discourse in Mark and Luke, Jesus used only one parable, the Parable of the Fig Tree.

A parable is an illustration, example, or incident of common knowledge or experience to explain a teaching, saying, or incident that is not common knowledge. Our Lord wanted the disciples, as well as those living in the end of the age, to fully understand His teachings concerning evidences of the approach, or dawning, of "the great and terrible day of the Lord." The reason for the Olivet Discourse parables is given in 2 Peter 3:9-10, *"The Lord is not slack concerning his promise, as some men count slackness; but is longsuffering to usward, not willing that any should perish, but that all should come to repentance. But the day of the Lord will come as a thief in the night. . . ."*

There are excellent prophetic teachers who end the Olivet Discourse in Matthew at the end of chapter 24; thus, applying the last three parables found in chapter 25 to the church age of the dispensation of grace. We certainly have no problem with this particular application, but we understand the message of the Olivet Discourse in

Matthew to continue through chapter 25. Matthew, by common agreement, is Jewish and kingdom age; therefore we conclude if the parables of Matthew 25 were teachings for the Gentile church age, then they would have been placed in Luke. Again, we point out that this is our own conclusion and is not meant in any way to be critical of those who give the alternative explanation.

THE PARABLE OF THE FIG TREE

We have already discussed the first parable to some extent, but we will briefly consider it again. It is mentioned in Matthew 24:32-36:

> *"Now learn a parable of the fig tree; When his branch is yet tender, and putteth forth leaves, ye know that summer is nigh: So likewise ye, when ye shall see all these things, know that it is near, even at the doors. Verily I say unto you, This generation shall not pass, till all these things be fulfilled. Heaven and earth shall pass away, but my words shall not pass away. But of that day and hour knoweth no man, no, not the angels of heaven, but my Father only."*

As already stated, the gospel of Matthew is Jewish in intent and application. Likewise, the Olivet Discourse as recorded in Matthew is oriented to God's dealing with Israel in the latter days, during the Tribulation, and in the kingdom age. In Matthew 24:30 Jesus refers to the tribes of the earth, meaning the tribes of God's earthly people Israel, mourning for Him as they see the Son of man coming in the clouds of Heaven. In Zechariah 12:10 we read of this event to come, when Israel recognizes Jesus Christ as the Messiah: *"And I will pour upon the house of David, and upon the inhabitants of Jerusalem, the spirit of grace and of supplications: and they shall look upon me whom they have pierced, and they shall mourn for him, as one mourneth for his only son. . . ."*

In Matthew 24:31 Jesus speaks of sending His angels to gather together His elect, meaning Israel, from one end of Heaven to the other. Israel is God's earthly elect nation, and the church is God's elect heavenly body. We read of the regathering of Israel in Jeremiah 23:6,8, *"In his days Judah shall be saved, and Israel shall dwell safely: and this is his name whereby he shall be called, **the Lord our righteousness** . . . The Lord liveth, which brought up and which led the seed of the house of Israel out of the north country, and from all countries whither I had driven them; and they shall dwell in their own land."*

Israel is dealt with, throughout the Olivet Discourse and even in the parables, as God's prophetic timepiece for the end of the age. Therefore, it should be evident to every student of prophecy that the fig tree of the first parable is symbolic of Israel. In Scripture, the fig tree is representative of national Israel, the olive tree speaks of spiritual Israel, and the vine refers to messianic Israel, spreading the message of salvation in the Redeemer to all nations. In Habakkuk 3:17 we read of Israel's being cut off in the days of her dispersion, *". . . the fig tree shall not blossom, neither shall fruit be in the vines; the labour of the olive shall fail. . . ."* In Matthew 21:18-22 we read of the cursing of the fig tree by Jesus. The fig tree had abundant leaves, but no fruit for the Lord, so Jesus put a curse upon it, and it withered and died. This practical example demonstrated God's displeasure with Israel, and in 70 A.D. Israel as a nation died and withered away. This cursing of the fig tree was spelled out in literal language by Jesus in the temple, just before He departed to Mt. Olivet. We read in Matthew 23:33,36, *"Ye serpents, ye generation of vipers, how can ye escape the damnation of hell? . . . Verily I say unto you, All these things shall come upon this generation."* All that Jesus prophesied for that generation of Israel came to pass. Most of those to whom Jesus spoke, those who were thirty years of age or under, saw the destruction of Jerusalem and the temple, and the death of Israel as a nation.

But in the next chapter, Matthew 24, Jesus spoke of the rebudding of the fig tree and of another generation,

The fig tree is not only identified as Israel scripturally, but also agriculturally. Fig trees grow to a larger size in Israel than any other country, often to heights of forty feet or more.

THE PARABLE OF THE DAYS OF NOAH

The second parable in the Olivet Discourse is given in Matthew 24:37-44:

"But as the days of Noe were, so shall also the coming of the Son of man be. For as in the days that were before the flood they were eating and drinking, marrying and giving in marriage, until the day that Noe entered into the ark, And knew not until the flood came, and took them all away; so shall also the coming of the Son of man

be. Then shall two be in the field; the one shall be taken, and the other left. Two women shall be grinding at the mill; the one shall be taken, and the other left. Watch therefore: for ye know not what hour your Lord doth come. But know this, that if the goodman of the house had known in what watch the thief would come, he would have watched, and would not have suffered his house to be broken up. Therefore be ye also ready: for in such an hour as ye think not the Son of man cometh."

The first item of importance in this parable is the status of the social order before the flood. When Jesus stated that the Antediluvians were engaged in eating, drinking, marrying, etc., He did not mean that they were simply carrying on normal, everyday pursuits of life. They were doing much more — engaging in sexual orgies, perversion, robbery, assault, rape, and every criminal act that could be imagined. In the New Testament we are informed concerning the last days, that people would again be seduced by spirits, committing vile abominations of every description, and iniquity would increase over the face of the earth (1 Tim. 4:1; 2 Tim. 3:1-7; 2 Thess. 2:6-12). The days of Noah are here again, as a witness that another world judgment is coming soon, and this is the way Jesus said it would be at the time of His return.

We also read in Genesis 6:1 that in the days before the flood there was a great population explosion. Man multiplied all over the face of the earth, and when man suffers from overcrowded living conditions, sin is more prevalent, and humans become utterly corrupt.

God's blessing upon the man and woman after they were created was to *". . . Be fruitful, and multiply, and replenish the earth . . ."* (Gen. 1:28). With people living almost a thousand years, still bearing children, it has been estimated by some that by the time the flood came there must have been fifteen billion people living on earth. The example in China where a family unit is prohibited by law in producing more than one offspring is another indication that we are again living in the "days of Noah."

We read in Isaiah 5:8,11-12,14, *"Woe unto them that join house to house, that lay field to field, till there be no place, that they may be placed alone in the midst of the earth! . . . Woe unto them that rise up early in the morning, that they may follow strong drink; that continue until night, till wine inflame them! And the harp, and the viol, the tabret, and pipe, and wine, are in their feasts: but they regard not the work of the Lord, neither consider the operation of his hands . . . Therefore hell hath enlarged herself, and opened her mouth without measure: and their glory, and their multitude, and their pomp, and he that rejoiceth, shall descend into it."*

Isaiah said that when there is a population explosion, and the thoughts of men are continually on alcohol, drugs, pleasure, and sex, Hell enlarges itself to receive the souls of the millions who plunge into it. Hell cannot be filled up, because God made it so that it could enlarge itself.

As it was before the flood, there is a population explosion. In order to try to control it, contraceptive devices and birth control pills of every description are being produced. Birth control pills for men are now being manufactured. The more pills that are produced, the more sex is glorified and promiscuity is encouraged. This leads to more abortions and more venereal disease among the young people. Even so, the population continues to increase, until in some parts of the world it will soon be "standing room only." It is as it was in the days of Noah.

Scriptural evidence indicates that the Antediluvians scoffed and mocked the preaching of Noah concerning the coming flood, and again we see the unbelieving spirit of the masses and the apostate religious element present in our day. We read in 2 Peter 3:3-4, *"Knowing this first, that there shall come in the last days scoffers, walking after their own lusts, And saying, Where is the promise of his coming? for since the fathers fell asleep, all things continue as they were from the beginning of the creation. For this they willingly are ignorant of. . . ."*

Even before Noah, Enoch preached to the Antediluvians that God's judgment would come upon them for their ungodliness. Enoch not only preached judgment in his generation, but he also looked forward about five thousand years to a similar generation that would likewise refuse to receive the mercy and grace of God, choosing rather to continue in their ungodly condition. Enoch speaks to this very generation in which we live. We read in Jude 14-15, *"And Enoch also, the seventh from Adam, prophesied of these, saying, Behold, the Lord cometh with ten thousands of his saints, To execute judgment upon all, and to convince all that are ungodly among them of all their ungodly deeds which they have ungodly committed, and of all their hard speeches which ungodly sinners have spoken against him."*

Some five thousand years ago God revealed to the patriarch Enoch the exceeding sinfulness that would be prevalent in our generation, and Enoch wept for the billions living today who are on their way to Hell. Jesus said that as it was in the days of Noah, so it will be when He comes again. The unregenerate, pleasure-seeking masses will refuse to believe the message of God's servants, until the judgment comes and takes them all away. But praise God, the grace of God is still available to all who will believe on the Lord Jesus Christ and be saved.

THE PARABLE OF ONE TAKEN, ONE LEFT

The third parable in the Olivet Discourse is given in Matthew 24:40-41:

"Then shall two be in the field; the one shall be taken, and the other left. Two women shall be grinding at the mill; the one shall be taken, and the other left. Watch therefore: for ye know not what hour your Lord doth come."

In this parable about the two women in the field, and the two women at the mill, was Jesus in any way referring to the Rapture of the church? There is nothing in this parable directly related to the translation of the church, which occurs before the Great Tribulation begins. Certainly, we believe that Jesus will come in the air and catch away all Christians, the living and those who sleep in their grave, before the judgments of the Great Tribulation fall. Like Enoch, Christians will be translated, but the parable of the two women has no relation to the Rapture for the following reasons:

1. The subject here is judgment, not salvation. We read in

the preceding verses that the flood came and took the ungodly away. Likewise, when Jesus comes at the end of the Tribulation, two women will be in the field, and one will be taken in judgment and the other left. Two women will be grinding at the mill, and one will be taken away in judgment, and the other left. The greatest judgments of the Great Tribulation will come at the end when Christ returns: great earthquakes, the battle of Armageddon, and terrible cosmic upheavals.

2. We read again Matthew 24:39-40, "*. . . so shall also the coming of the **Son of man** be. **Then** shall two be in the field; the one shall be taken, and the other left.*" The title of Jesus as He comes back all the way to the earth to rule and reign over the nations is always given as the "Son of man." Jesus is never called the "Son of man" in His saving and keeping power over the church; He is never referred to as the "Son of man" as He comes for the church in the air. He comes back to reign on David's throne as the "Son of man." But to the church, citizens of Heaven, He is the "Son of God" with power. We read in the parable of the two sets of two women that at the "coming of the Son of man" at the end of the Tribulation, **then** (meaning at that time) one-half of all remaining alive will be taken away in judgment, as the ungodly were taken away in the flood.

During our recent tour of Israel, it was called to our attention that Israeli men and women generally work in pairs. When you look in the fields, you will usually see two women gathering tomatoes or some other fruit or vegetable, or two men plowing or planting together. Evidently this is a Hebrew custom that is thousands of years old. Thus, this is added evidence that this parable is for Israel, and not for the church. All scriptures relating to the Rapture, the translation of the church, emphasize salvation. Those referring to the literal return of Jesus as King of kings stress judgment.

THE PARABLE OF THE THIEF

In Matthew 24:42-44, Jesus compared His return at the end of the Tribulation to a thief coming in the night:

"Watch therefore: for ye know not what hour your Lord doth come. But know this, that if the goodman of the house had known in what watch the thief would come, he would have watched, and would not have suffered his house to be broken up. Therefore be ye also ready: for in such an hour as ye think not the Son of man cometh."

In the Old Testament the night is divided into three watches: from 6:00 p.m. until midnight, from midnight until 3:00 a.m., and from 3:00 a.m. until 6:00 p.m. In the New Testament, the night is divided into four equal segments. Guards were placed on the walls of the city, or at important places, to protect the citizens from a surprise attack.

It will be especially important for Israelites during the last half of the Great Tribulation to understand that the Messiah is coming, and to be ready to receive Him. Jesus Himself said, in looking forward to His coming again: *"Behold, your house is left unto you desolate. For I say unto you, Ye shall not see me henceforth, till ye shall say, Blessed is he that cometh in the name of the Lord"* (Matt. 23:38-39). We read also of His glorious appearing to Israel in Romans 11:26-27, *"And so all Israel shall be saved: as it is written, There shall come out of Sion the Deliverer, and shall turn away ungodliness from Jacob: For this is my covenant unto them, when I shall take away their sins."*

Only those Israelites who are ready and spiritually prepared to receive Jesus Christ as the promised Messiah and Redeemer will be saved. All others will be cut off. Zechariah 13:8-9 says, *"And it shall come to pass, that in all the land, saith the Lord, two parts therein shall be cut off and die; but the third shall be left therein. And I will bring the third part through the fire, and will refine them as silver is refined, and will try them as gold is tried: they shall call on my name, and I will hear them: I will say, It is my people: and they shall say, The Lord is my God."*

The parable of the thief was given especially for the Jews living in the last half of the Tribulation, because the time of the Lord's coming is given in terms of hours, not seasons or days. Also, we note again the wording of verse 42, *"Watch therefore: for ye know not what hour your Lord doth come."* Jesus did not say, what hour your Lord **will** come, or **shall** come. He said, **doth** come — the verb form here is present tense, or near present tense. Also, notice again the wording of verse 44, *"Therefore be ye also ready: for in such an hour as ye think not the Son of man cometh."* The verb form here is in the present tense also. The parable of the thief in the Olivet Discourse is to be connected directly to the warning of Revelation 16:15-16, *"Behold, I come as a thief. Blessed is he that watcheth,* *and keepeth his garments, lest he walk naked, and they see his shame. And he gathered them together into a place called in the Hebrew tongue Armageddon."* Notice again the verb forms: **I come — Blessed is he that watcheth — Keepeth his garments — They see his shame —** All verb forms are in the present tense. It will indeed be a terrible day at that time, when Jesus Christ comes back with the armies of Heaven, for all who are not waiting and watching for His return.

Therefore, the parable of the thief was given for the enlightenment of those living at the time our Lord returns in judgment at the end of the Tribulation. But notice the application of this teaching for Christians in 1 Thessalonians 5:1-3, *"But of the times and the seasons, brethren, ye have no need that I write unto you. For yourselves know perfectly that the **day of the Lord** so cometh as a thief in the night. For when they shall say, Peace and safety; then sudden destruction cometh upon them, as travail upon a woman with child; and they shall not escape."*

The "day of the Lord" begins with the Rapture of the church, and more specifically, with the Tribulation period. We are admonished to be observing the signs of the times and seasons as the "day of the Lord," the Tribulation, approaches.

THE PARABLE OF THE TWO SERVANTS

The fifth parable in the Olivet Discourse is the one bout two servants, in Matthew 24:45-51:

"Who then is a faithful and wise servant, whom

his lord hath made ruler over his household, to give them meat in due season? Blessed is that servant, whom his lord when he cometh shall find so doing. Verily I say unto you, That he shall make him ruler over all his goods. But and if that evil servant shall say in his heart, My lord delayeth his coming; And shall begin to smite his fellow-servants, and to eat and drink with the drunken; The lord of that servant shall come . . . when he looketh not for him, and in an hour that he is not aware of, And shall cut him asunder, and appoint him his portion with the hypocrites: there shall be weeping and gnashing of teeth."

We should keep in mind that the entire context of the Olivet Discourse concerns the return of Jesus Christ and world conditions as they will be at that time. The parable of the two servants, like the other parables of Matthew 24 and 25, is to be interpreted in this light. Of the two servants, like the two women grinding at the mill, one was taken in judgment, and one was welcomed into the kingdom. William L. Pettingill said of the two servants:

"They do not touch on salvation by faith of those who believe during the present dispensation. Nothing is more clearly taught in the epistles than that every Christian will be caught up at the Rapture. This is a part of our salvation, and salvation is never a matter of rewards or deserving, but only of grace."

The choosing of two servants to illustrate this parable also signifies that it has special reference to Jewish discipleship. We read in Isaiah 41:8, *"But thou, Israel, art my servant. . . ."* Christians are members of God's family by adoption.

This parable also teaches the importance of enduring to the end during the Tribulation. In the Olivet Discourse, Jesus previously said in Matthew 24:12-13, *"And because iniquity shall abound, the love of many shall wax cold. But he that shall endure unto the end, the same shall be saved."* We read in Revelation that if any man, Gentile or Israelite, were to weaken and worship the Antichrist or take his mark, he would be eternally damned. During the Tribulation only those who endure to the end — although some will suffer martyrdom — will be saved. But it is apparent from Daniel 9:27 that many Jews will be deceived. Those who endure will be appointed rulers over the kingdom of Jesus Christ here on earth, as with the faithful servants in the parable. We read of them in Revelation 20:4, *"And I saw thrones, and they sat upon them, and judgment was given unto them: and I saw the souls of them that were beheaded for the witness of Jesus, and for the word of God, and which had not worshipped the beast, neither his image, neither had received his mark upon their foreheads, or in their hands; and they lived and reigned with Christ a thousand years."*

The unfaithful servant, who is cut asunder in the day the Lord comes, will be given his lot with the hypocrites spoken of in the previous chapter. Jesus said of them in Mattew 23:29,33, *". . . hypocrites . . . Ye serpents, ye generation of vipers, how can ye escape the damnation of hell?"* They will be cut off from the kingdom and cast into outer darkness, where there shall be weeping and gnashing of teeth. This lesson in faithfulness during the Great Tribulation is also given in Matthew 13:49-50, *"So shall it be at the end of the world* [meaning age]: *the angels shall come forth, and sever the wicked from among the just, And shall cast them into the furnace of fire: there shall be wailing and gnashing of teeth."*

The lesson for us in the parables of the Olivet Discourse is to be ready for the translation of Christians out of this world to escape the Great Tribulation, should the "day of the Lord" come in our lifetime. God instructs all in His Word, the Bible, that if they will acknowledge to Him their lost condition, and receive Jesus Christ as the Son of God who died for their sins, they will be saved.

THE PARABLE OF THE TEN VIRGINS

The sixth parable is recorded in Matthew 25:1-13:

"Then shall the kingdom of heaven be likened unto ten virgins, which took their lamps, and went forth to meet the bridegroom. And five of them were wise, and five were foolish. They that were foolish took their lamps, and took no oil with them: But the wise took oil in their vessels with their lamps. While the bridegroom tarried, they all slumbered and slept. And at midnight there was a cry made, Behold, the bridegroom cometh; go ye out to meet him. Then all those virgins arose, and trimmed their lamps. And the foolish said unto the wise, Give us of your oil; for our lamps are gone out. But the wise

*answered, saying, Not so, lest there be not
enough for us and you: but go ye rather to them
that sell, and buy for yourselves. And while they
went to buy, the bridegroom came; and they
that were ready went in with him to the marriage:
and the door was shut. Afterward came also the
other virgins, saying, Lord, Lord, open to us.
But he answered and said, Verily I say unto you,
I know you not. Watch therefore, for ye know
neither the day nor the hour wherein the Son of
man cometh."*

In the Bible, chastity and purity are equated with
spirituality. False religious systems are compared to
adulterous women. In verse 1 of the parable we read
again, *"Then shall the kingdom of heaven be likened unto
ten virgins, which took their lamps, and went forth to
meet the bridegroom."* The ten virgins represent those of
Israel at the second coming of Jesus Christ who profess a
belief in Him as the Messiah, because they all go out to
meet the bridgeroom. The Syriac text reads that the ten
virgins went out to meet the Bridegroom and the Bride.
But in any event, where the Bridegroom is, there is the
Bride also. They took their lamps, because in traditional
Jewish weddings the celebration began after the marriage
ceremony, when the even star appeared in the sky. The
time would be somewhere between 8:00 and 10:00 in the
evening, depending upon the season of the year. The bride
selected a delegation of intimate friends to accompany the
bridegroom to her house. The delegation of bridesmaids
is represented by the ten virgins. The ten virgins are not
the bride. They represent the friends of the bride who go

in with the bridegroom to the marriage feast in her house. The delegation of bridesmaids took lamps because, as we have already brought out, the celebration took place at night. The lamps represent the Word of God: *"Thy word is a lamp unto my feet, and a light unto my path"* (Ps. 119:105).

In the Scriptures, the Tribulation is referred to as the night of human history, and Jesus Christ will come as a thief in the night. Only those who have the Word of God to guide them during the Tribulation will find salvation and be saved. We read in Revelation 6:9, *". . . I saw under the altar the souls of them that were slain for the word of God, and for the testimony which they held."*

The bridegroom of the parable represented the Lord Jesus Christ. The marriage has already occurred, and we read of it in Revelation 19:7-9, *"Let us be glad and rejoice, and give honour to him: for the marriage of the Lamb is come, and his wife hath made herself ready. And to her was granted that she should be arrayed in fine linen, clean and white: for the fine linen is the righteousness of saints. And he saith unto me, Write, Blessed are they which are called unto the marriage supper of the Lamb. . . ."*

The scene described is a heavenly one. The Lamb, the Lord Jesus Christ, claims His Bride, and she stands before Him in robes of righteousness without spot or wrinkle. We believe the Bride to be the church, which is caught up to be with Jesus just before the Tribulation begins. We read in Ephesians 5:25-27, *". . . Christ also loved the church, and gave himself for it; That he might sanctify and cleanse it with the washing of water by the word, That he might present it to himself a glorious church, not having spot, or wrinkle, or any such thing; but that it should be holy and without blemish."*

The bridegroom did not appear early in the evening as the ten virgins had expected, and as the hours dragged by, they slumbered and slept. Throughout the Olivet Discourse Jesus repeated the warning that those in the Tribulation should be watching, lest they faint, fall asleep, and not endure unto the end. Some will slumber and get lost in the night by letting their lamps go out. Some will follow the false Christ, the false bridegroom, and we read in Matthew 24:26-27. *"Wherefore if they shall say unto you, Behold, he is in the desert; go not forth: behold he is in the secret chambers; believe it not. For as the lightning cometh out of the east, and shineth even unto the west; so shall also the coming of the Son of man be."*

Oil in the Bible, and especially refined oil of the olive tree, is representative of the Holy Spirit, just as the olive tree is symbolic of spiritual Israel. The oil of the olive was used in lamps. Five of the virgins took only the oil in their lamps. Eventually their lamps went out, and they had no extra oil to relight them. But five of the virgins made provisions for the contingency that the bridegroom might be later in coming than they thought, so these took along extra containers of oil.

The scene at midnight, when the heralder of the wedding feast finally made the pronouncement, *"Behold, the bridegroom cometh . . .",* is a pitiful one. The five foolish virgins who took no extra oil could not light their lamps, and without light they could not accompany the bridegroom in to the wedding supper.

Jesus said that all whom God had given Him, He knew, and that all who came to Him by faith He would in no wise cast out. To make the ten virgins the church is to say that some will be saved and others will be lost, or that some will be taken in the Rapture and some left behind.

In the parable of the ten virgins, Jesus took an event that was common knowledge and common practice in Israel, a national custom and tradition still practiced today, to teach the Jews a truth about the bringing in of the kingdom of Heaven as His second coming. Jesus was simply illustrating to the Jews that only those in the Tribulation who endured until the end would be saved. Gentile believers have difficulty in interpreting this parable, because it is meant specifically for the Jews at the time of the coming of Christ to reign on earth, and we can be assured that many Jews during the Tribulation will heed its important message.

THE PARABLE OF THE TALENTS

The seventh parable of Jesus in the Olivet Discourse is the parable of the talents, in Matthew 25:14-30:

> *"For the kingdom of heaven is as a man travelling into a far country, who called his own servants, and delivered unto them his goods. And unto one he gave five talents, to another two, and to another one; to every man according to his several ability; and straightway took his journey. Then he that had received the five talents went and traded with the same, and made them other five talents. And likewise he that had received two, he also gained other two. But he that had received one went and digged the earth, and hid his lord's money. After a long*

time the lord of those servants cometh, and reckoneth with them. And so he that had received five talents came and brought other five talents, saying, Lord, thou deliverest unto me five talents: behold, I have gained beside them five talents more. His lord said unto him, Well done, thou good and faithful servant: thou hast been faithful over a few things, I will make thee ruler over many things: enter thou into the joy of thy lord. He also that had received two talents came and said, Lord, thou deliverest unto me two talents: behold, I have gained two other talents beside them. His lord said unto him, Well done, good and faithful servant; thou hast been faithful over a few things, I will make thee ruler over many things: enter thou into the joy of thy lord. Then he which had received the one talent came and said, Lord, I knew thee that thou art an hard man, reaping where thou hast not sown, and gathering where thou hast not strawed: And I was afraid, and went and hid thy talent in the earth: lo, there thou hast that is thine. His lord answered and said unto him, Thou wicked and slothful servant, thou knewest that I reap where I sowed not, and gather where I have not strawed: Thou oughtest therefore to have put my money to the exchangers, and then at my coming I should have received mine own with usury. Take therefore the talent from him, and give it unto him which hath ten talents. For unto every one that hath shall be given, and he shall have abundance: but from him that hath not shall be taken away even that which he hath. And cast ye the unprofitable servant into outer darkness: there shall be weeping and gnashing of teeth."

The first point we make about this parable is that it is within the context of the Olivet Discourse and should not apply directly to Christian salvation or service. If we attempt to apply it to the Christian's standing with Christ, then we have to conclude that it is necessary to produce good works in order to remain saved. In other words, works would become a part of redemption, because the unprofitable servant was cast into outer darkness where there is weeping and gnashing of teeth. This interpretation would be in violation of the gospel of Christ whereby we are saved. We read in Ephesians 2:8-9, *"For by grace are ye saved through faith; and that not of yourselves: it is the gift of God: Not of works, lest any man should boast."* The parable of the talents came after the apostles had been enlightened about the truth that Jesus must first go to the Father and then return before the kingdom would be established.

As great a work as John the Baptist did, his works will appear punt in light of the mighty work the servants of the Lord will do in the kingdom age. All rebellion against God will be put down, and there will be mighty miracles of healing: the deaf will hear, the lame will walk, the mute will speak, the deserts (not only in Israel, but all over the world) will blossom like a rose garden, and all nations will witness the mighty power of Jesus Christ working through His chosen servants.

We read of the mighty works that will be accomplished

by the servants of Jesus Christ during the Millennium in Isaiah 35:1-6, *"The wilderness and the solitary place shall be glad for them; and the desert shall rejoice, and blossom as the rose. It shall blossom abundantly, and rejoice even with joy and singing: the glory of Lebanon shall be given unto it, the excellency of Carmel and Sharon, they shall see the glory of the Lord, and the excellency of our God. Strengthen ye the weak hands, and confirm the feeble knees. Say to them that are of a fearful heart, Be strong, fear not: behold, your God will come with vengeance, even God with a recompense; he will come and save you. Then the eyes of the blind shall be opened, and the ears of the deaf shall be unstopped. Then shall the lame man leap as an hart, and the tongue of the dumb shall sing: for in the wilderness shall waters break out, and streams in the desert."*

Certainly the lesson contained within the parable of the talents can be applied to Christian service. The spiritual law, "to whom much is given, much is required," has always been true. However, Christian motivation for service is not the loss of salvation, but rather the love of our Lord and Savior.

THE PARABLE OF THE SHEEP AND GOATS

The eighth and final parable of the Olivet Discourse concerns the dividing of the goats from the sheep. Eight is the number of Jesus Christ, or the number of a new beginning. Therefore, we are given a hint that this parable looks beyond the Millennium to the new heavens and the new earth. The text is given in Matthew 25:31-46:

"When the Son of man shall come in his glory,

and all the holy angels with him, then shall he sit upon the throne of his glory: And before him shall be gathered all nations: and he shall separate them one from another, as a shepherd divideth his sheep from the goats: And he shall set the sheep on his right hand, but the goats on the left. Then shall the King say unto them on his right hand, Come, ye blessed of my Father, inherit the kingdom prepared for you from the foundation of the world: For I was an hungered, and ye gave me meat: I was thirsty, and ye gave me drink: I was a stranger, and ye took me in: Naked, and ye clothed me: I was sick, and ye visited me: I was in prison, and ye came unto me. Then shall the righteous answer him, saying, Lord, when saw we thee an hungered, and fed thee? or thirsty, and gave thee drink? When saw we thee a stranger and took thee in? or naked, and clothed thee? Or when saw we thee sick, or in prison, and came unto thee? And the King shall answer and say unto them, Verily I say unto you, Inasmuch as ye have done it unto one of the least of these my brethren, ye have done it unto me. Then shall he say also unto them on the left hand, Depart from me, ye cursed, into everlasting fire, prepared for the devil and his angels: For I was an hungered, and ye gave me no meat: I was thirsty, and ye gave me no drink: I was a stranger, and ye took me not in: naked, and ye clothed me not: sick, and in prison, and ye visited me not. Then shall they also answer him, saying, Lord, when saw we thee an hungered, or athirst, or a stranger, or naked, or sick, or in prison, and did not minister unto thee? Then shall he answer them, saying, Verily I say unto you, Inasmuch as ye did it not to one of the least of these, ye did it not to me. And these shall go away into everlasting punishment: but the righteous into life eternal."

This is another one of the parables of the Olivet Discourse that is greatly misunderstood and misapplied. The social gospel preachers of our day have taken it to promote so-called Christian socialism; that is, that the main responsibility of the Christian is to feed the poor and redistribute the wealth of the world. But this is not what Jesus referred to in this teaching.

As in the other parables of the Olivet Discourse, Jesus gave a simple illustration using elements with which the apostles were familiar, and to which they could relate. They had witnessed the separation of the sheep and the goats many times. Goats and sheep were allowed to feed together during the day, but they were always separated at night. Sheep are placid animals, and at night they usually lie down and calmly rest until the morning. Goats are more aggressive and restless at night, so they had to be separated. Jesus took the simple illustration of separating the sheep and the goats to teach the apostles what the kingdom of Heaven would be like in respect to nations when He came again.

To find the meaning of this parable and its proper application, let us study it in its different divisions. We read first Matthew 25:31, *"When the Son of man shall come in his glory, and all the holy angels with him, then shall he sit upon the throne of his glory."* Has Jesus come in His glory? Certainly not. During the kingdom age, all nations are to come up to Jerusalem to worship the King, and Israel is to be the head of the nations (Zech. 4:17-21; Isa. 60:9-22).

During the course of the kingdom age, when nations are judged concerning their relationship to Israel, the nations that continue to rebel against the King's authority will be cut off, and those which follow Him and accept the leadership of Israel will be spared. We read in Matthew 25:40, *". . . Inasmuch as ye have done it unto one of the least of these my brethren, ye have done it unto me."*

Dake's Annotated Reference Bible states concerning the explanation of this scripture: *". . . God will curse or bless according to how men have dealt with Israel. . . . This is the reason and basis for this judgment."*

It seems apparent from Scripture that this judgment of the nations on the basis of their relationship with Israel, the Lord's brethren according to the flesh, will come at the end of the kingdom age, and not at the beginning. Those nations that are destroyed at the end of the Millennium will be those nations which have rejected Israel and Israel's King, the Lord Jesus Christ. We read in Revelation 20:9, *"And they went up on the breadth of the earth, and compassed the camp of the saints about, and the beloved city* [Jerusalem]*: and fire came down from God out of heaven, and devoured them."*

We know from Revelation 20:1-7 that this will occur after the thousand-year reign of Jesus Christ as King of all nations. Those nations that are saved will inherit the new earth. We read of the new Jerusalem and the new earth in Revelation 21:24, *"And the nations of them which are saved shall walk in the light of it* [new Jerusalem] *and the kings of the earth do bring their glory and honour into it."*

This completes our study of the parables of the Olivet Discourse, and if we keep these teachings concerning the second coming of Christ, and Israel and the kingdom age in proper perspective, we have a consistent and composite picture of that great and wonderful day when Jesus will return to sit upon the throne of His glory.